This Mandala Book Belongs To

....

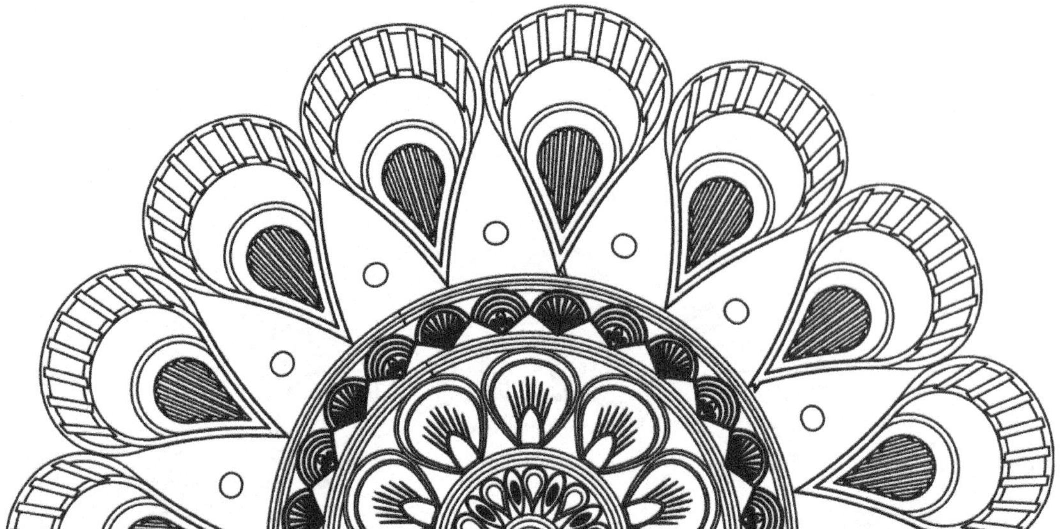

Mandala Coloring Book

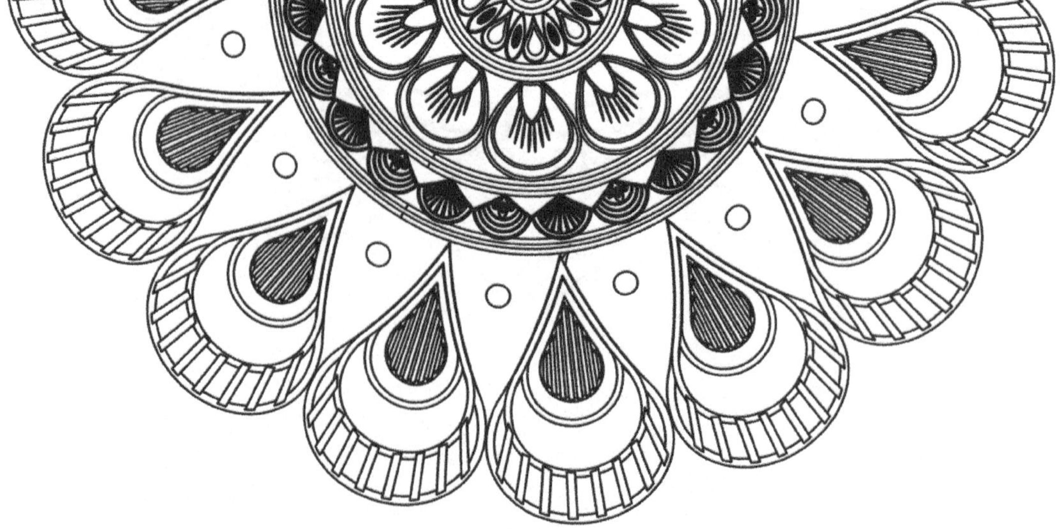

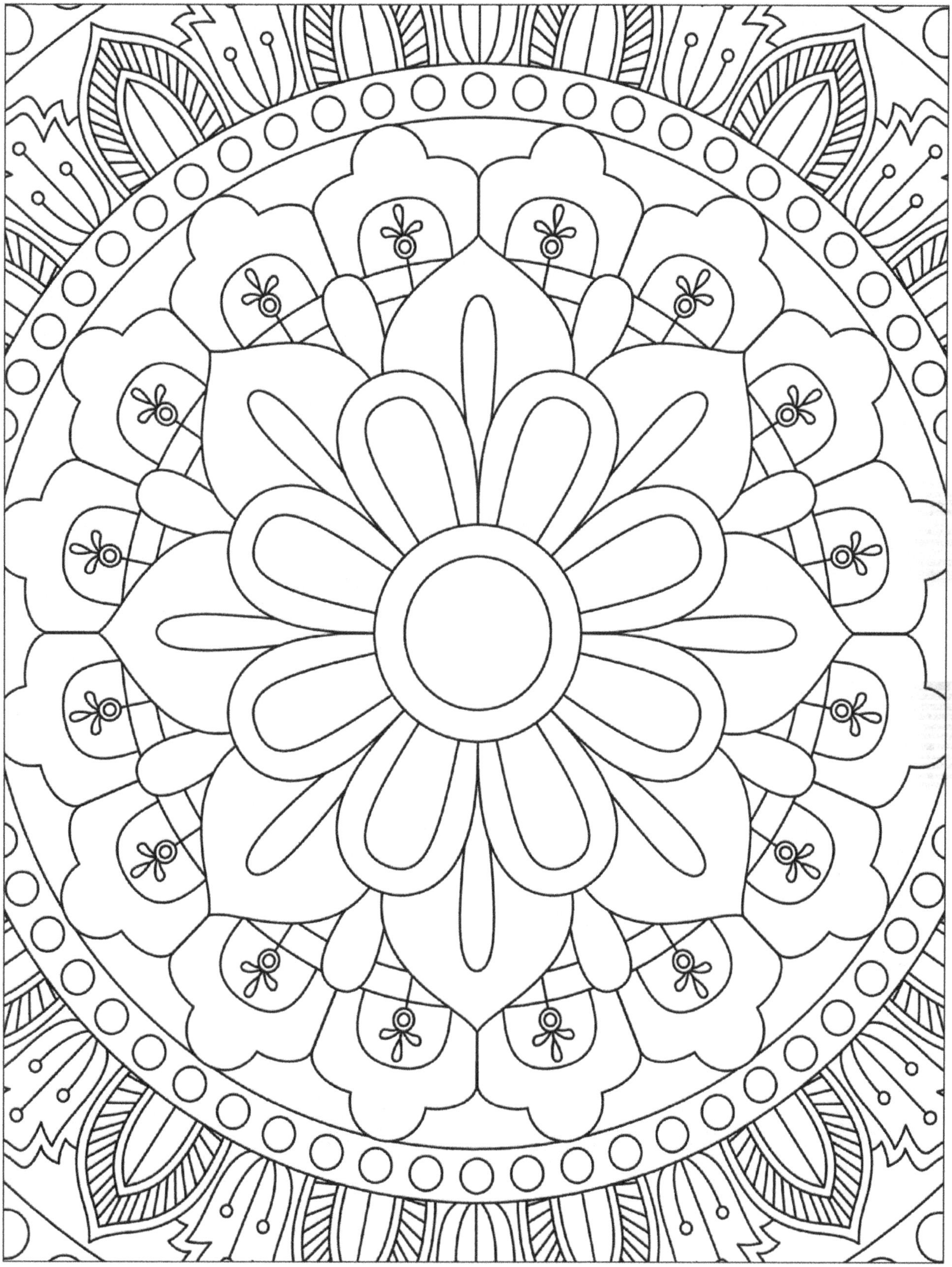

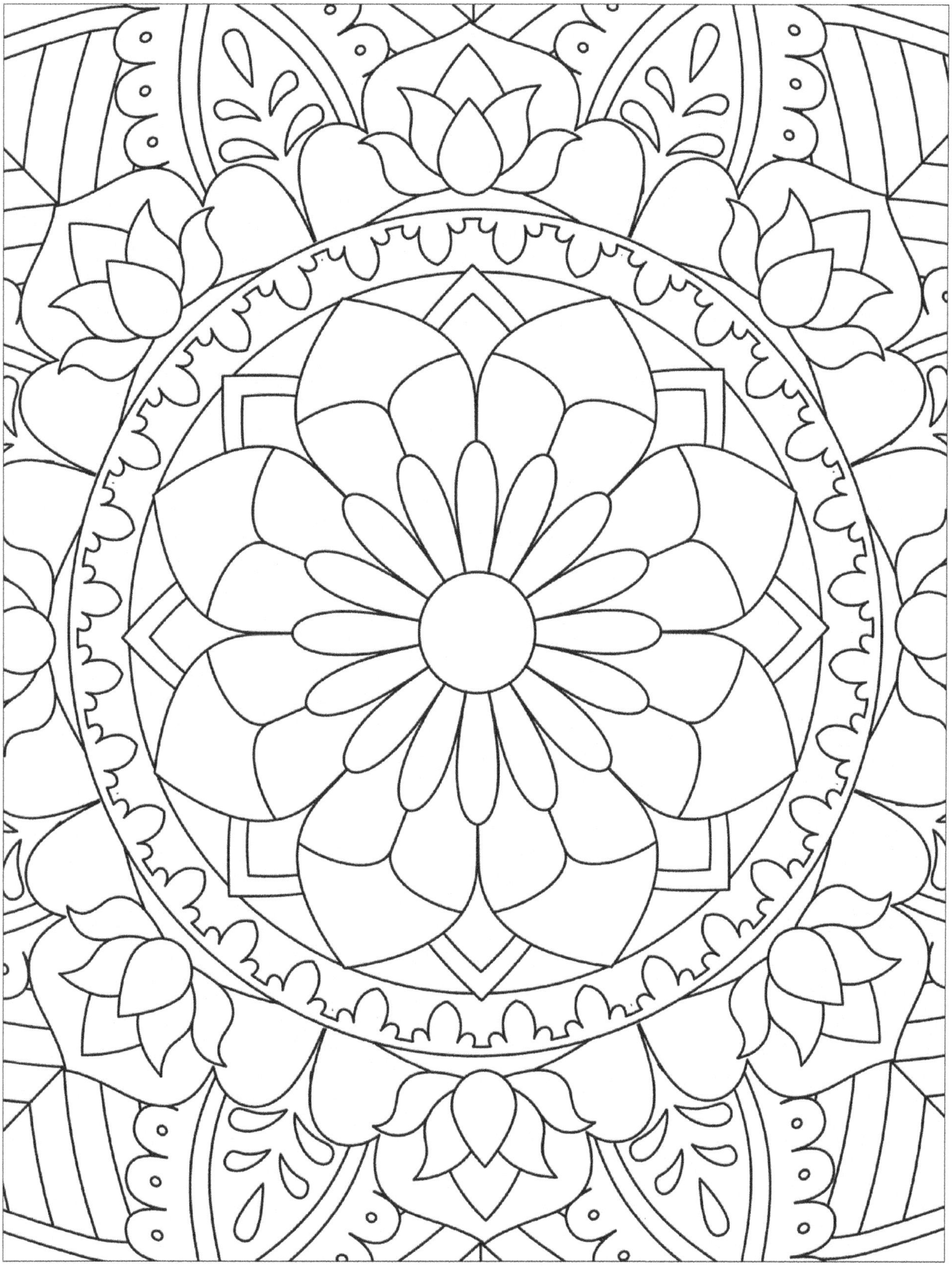

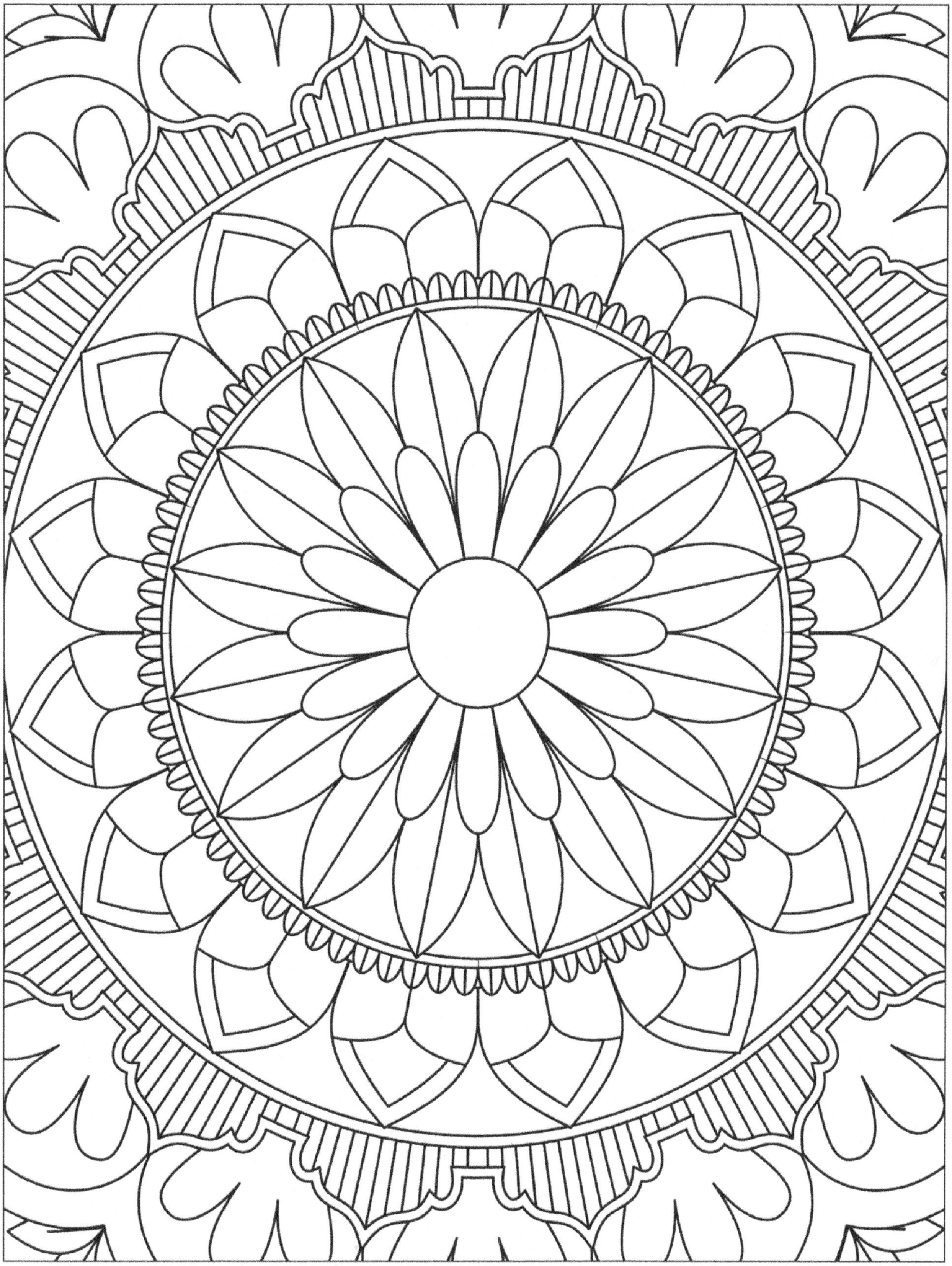

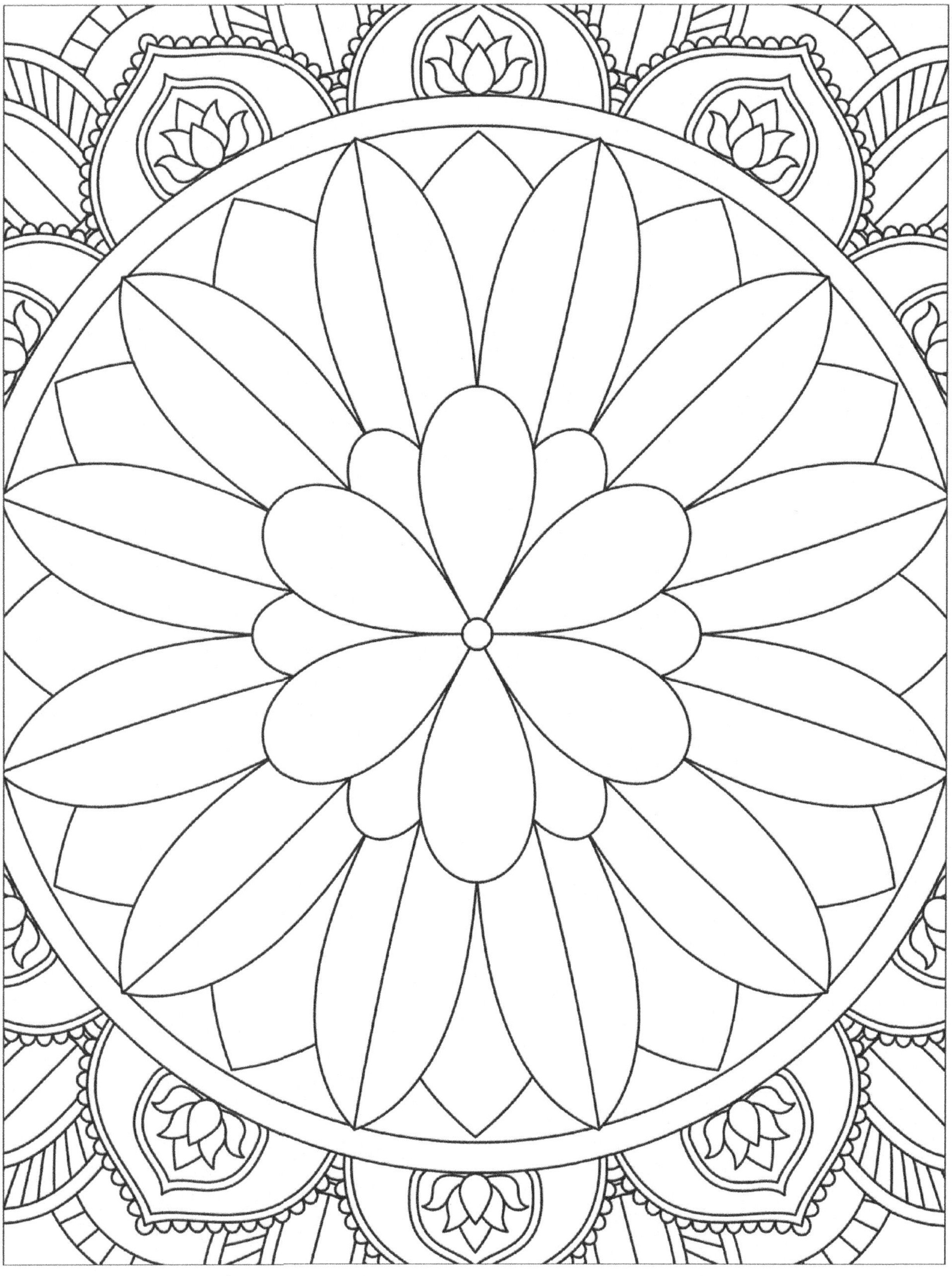

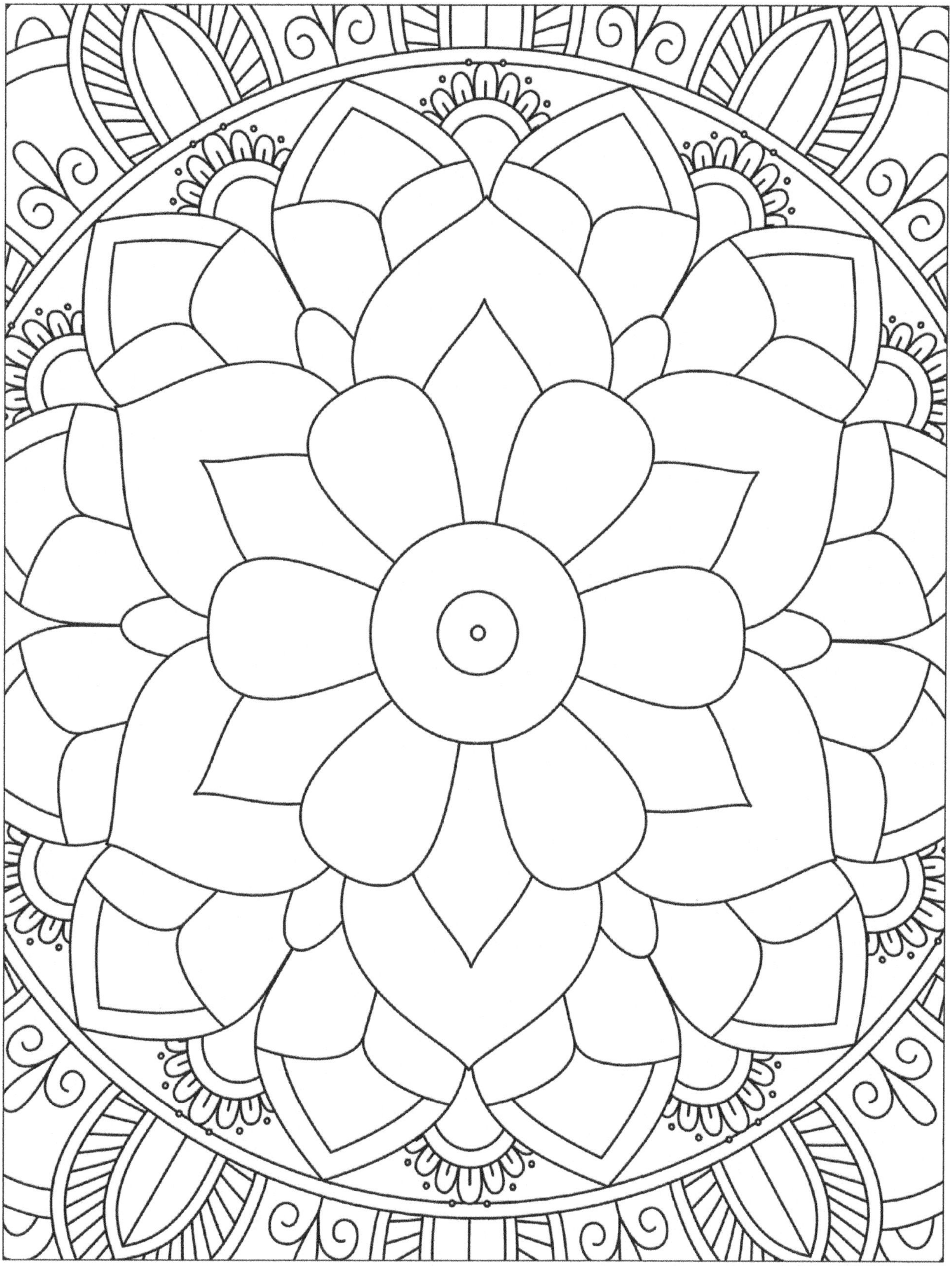

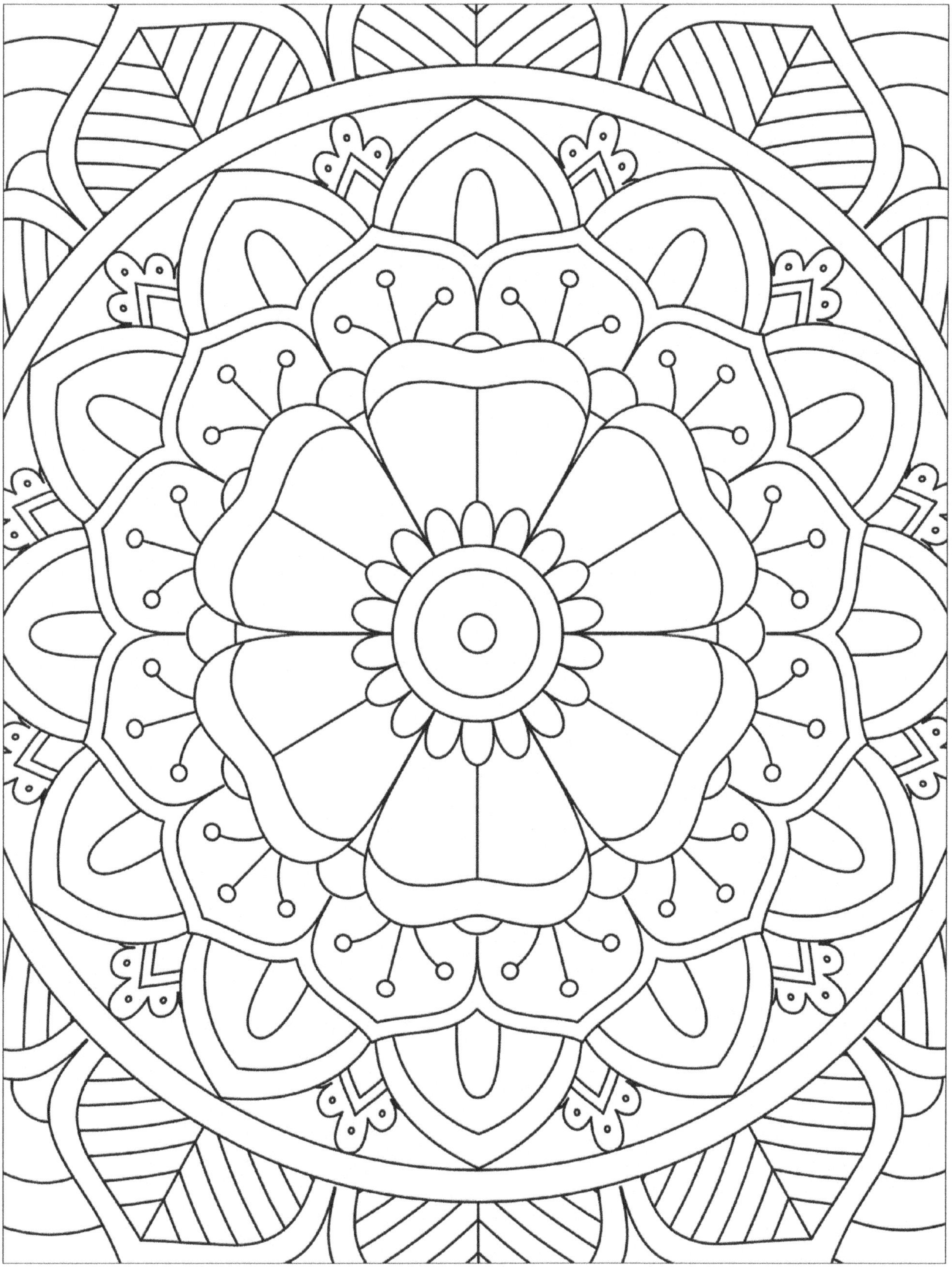

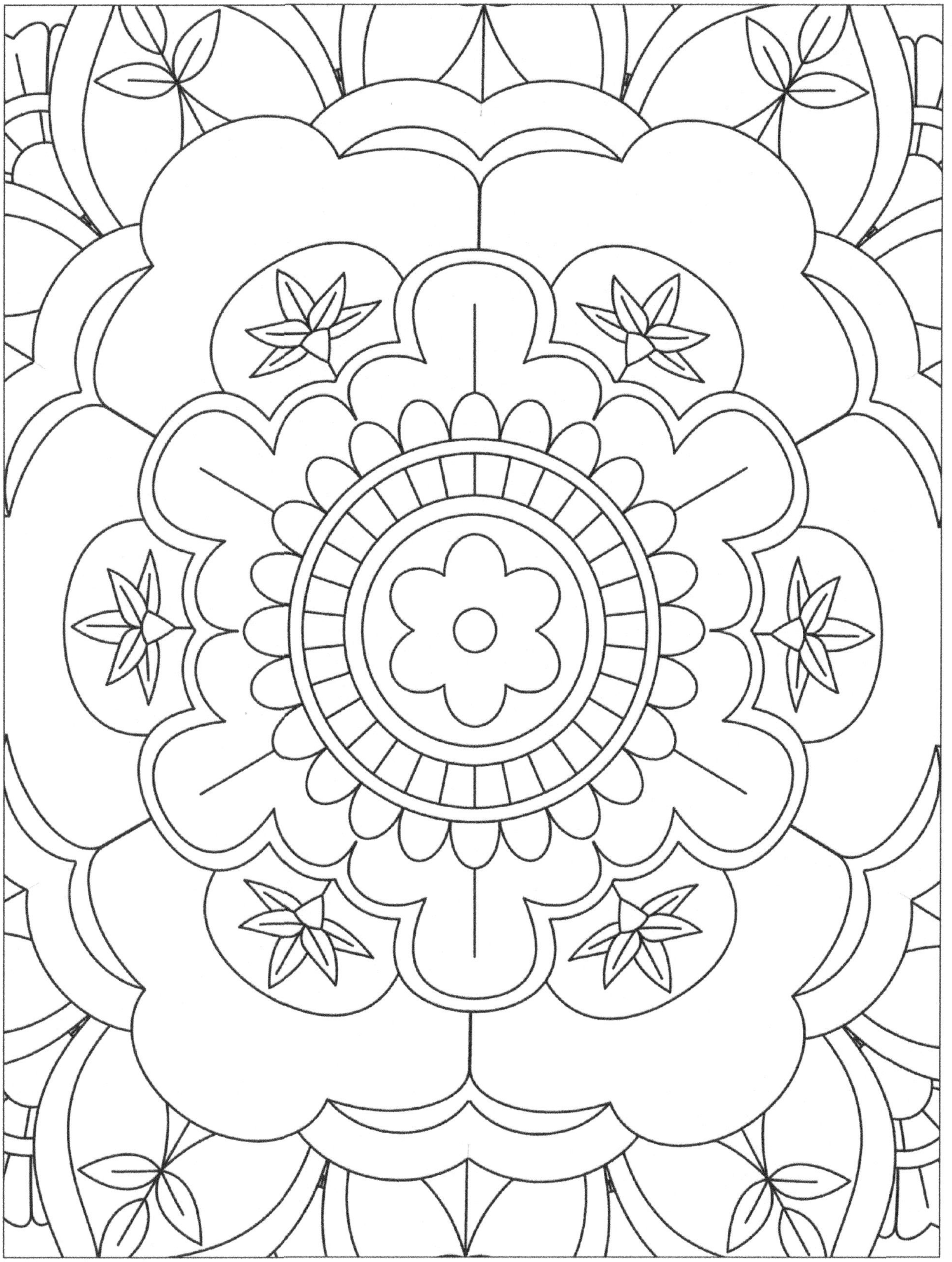

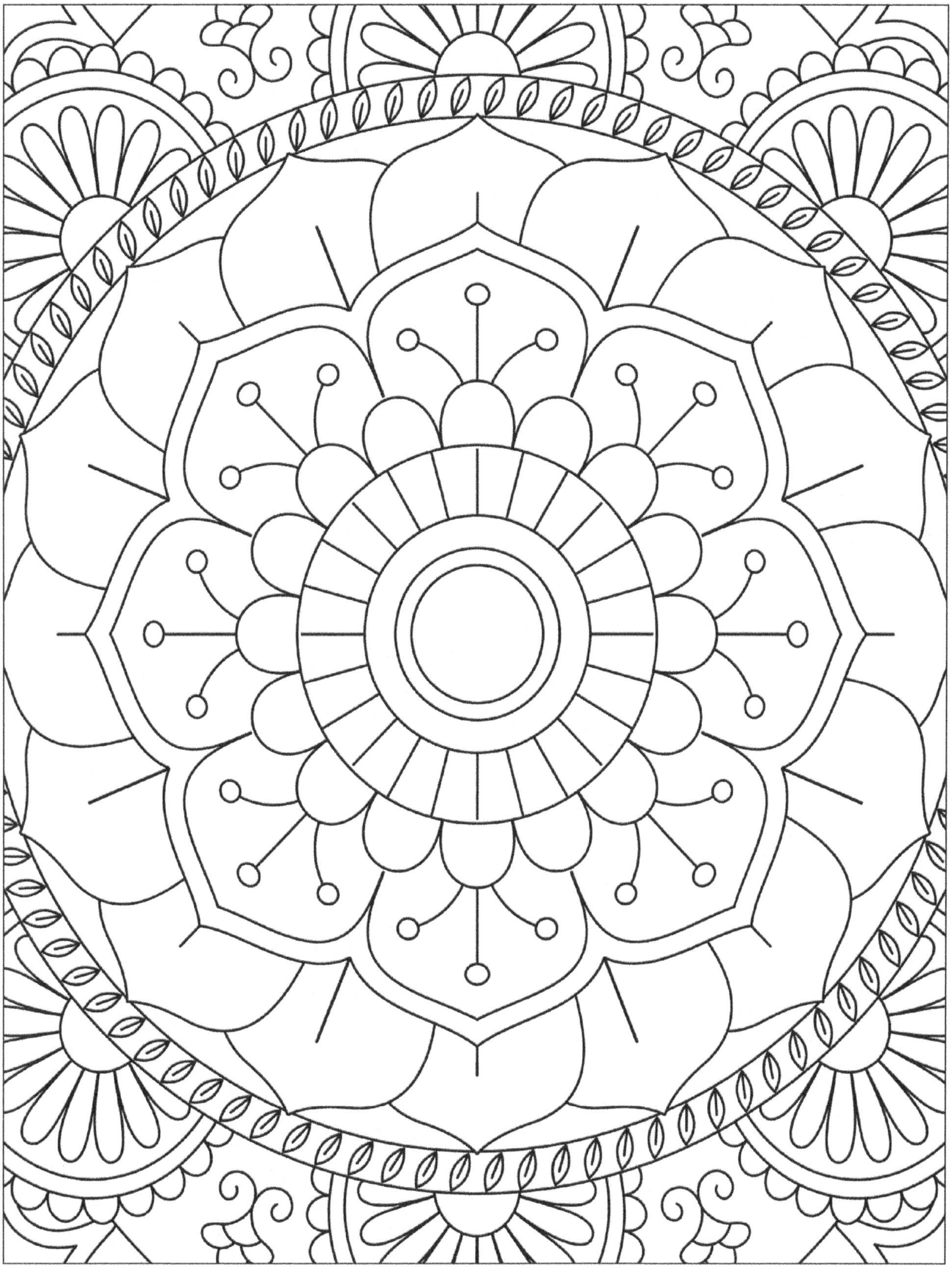

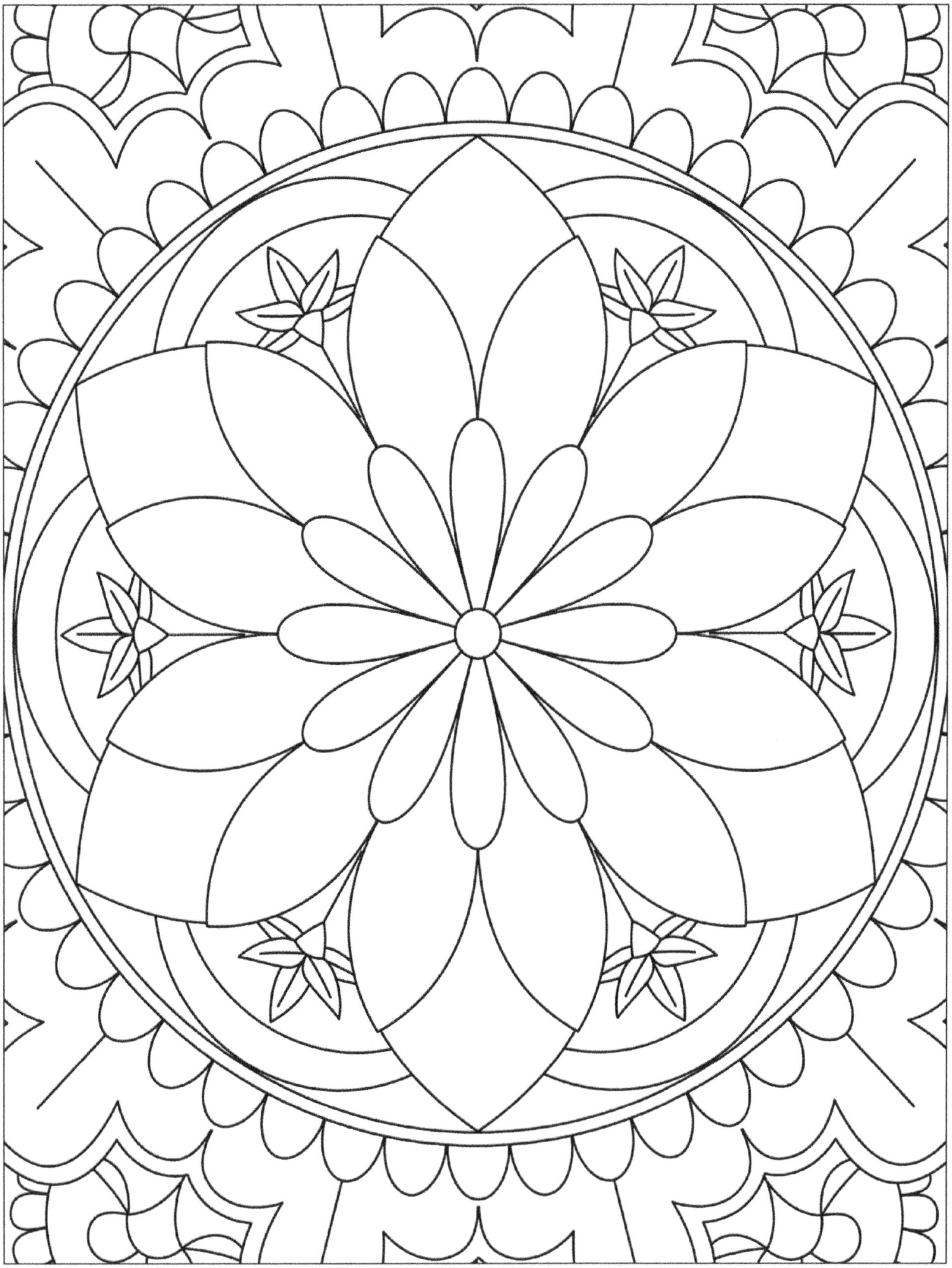

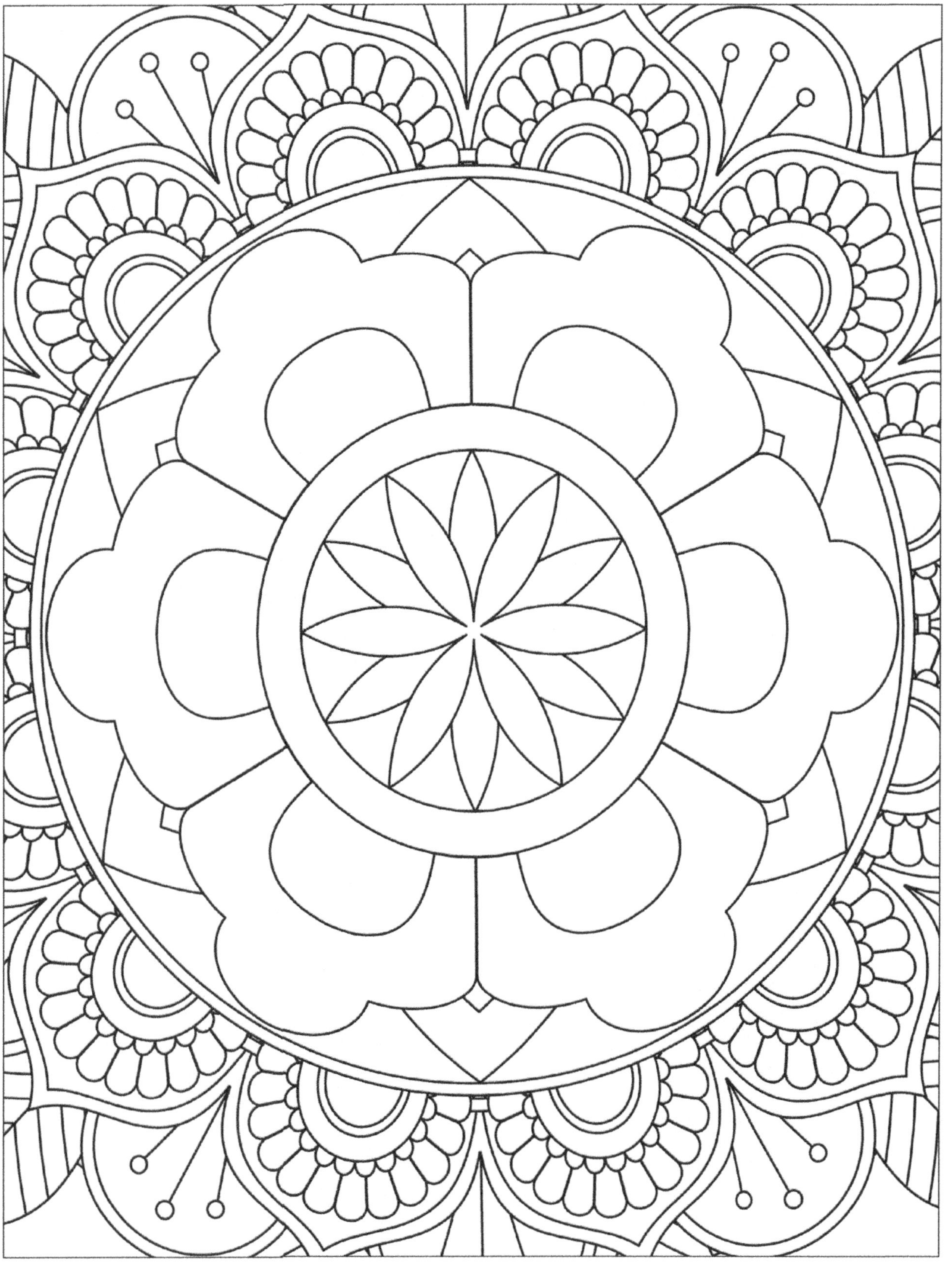

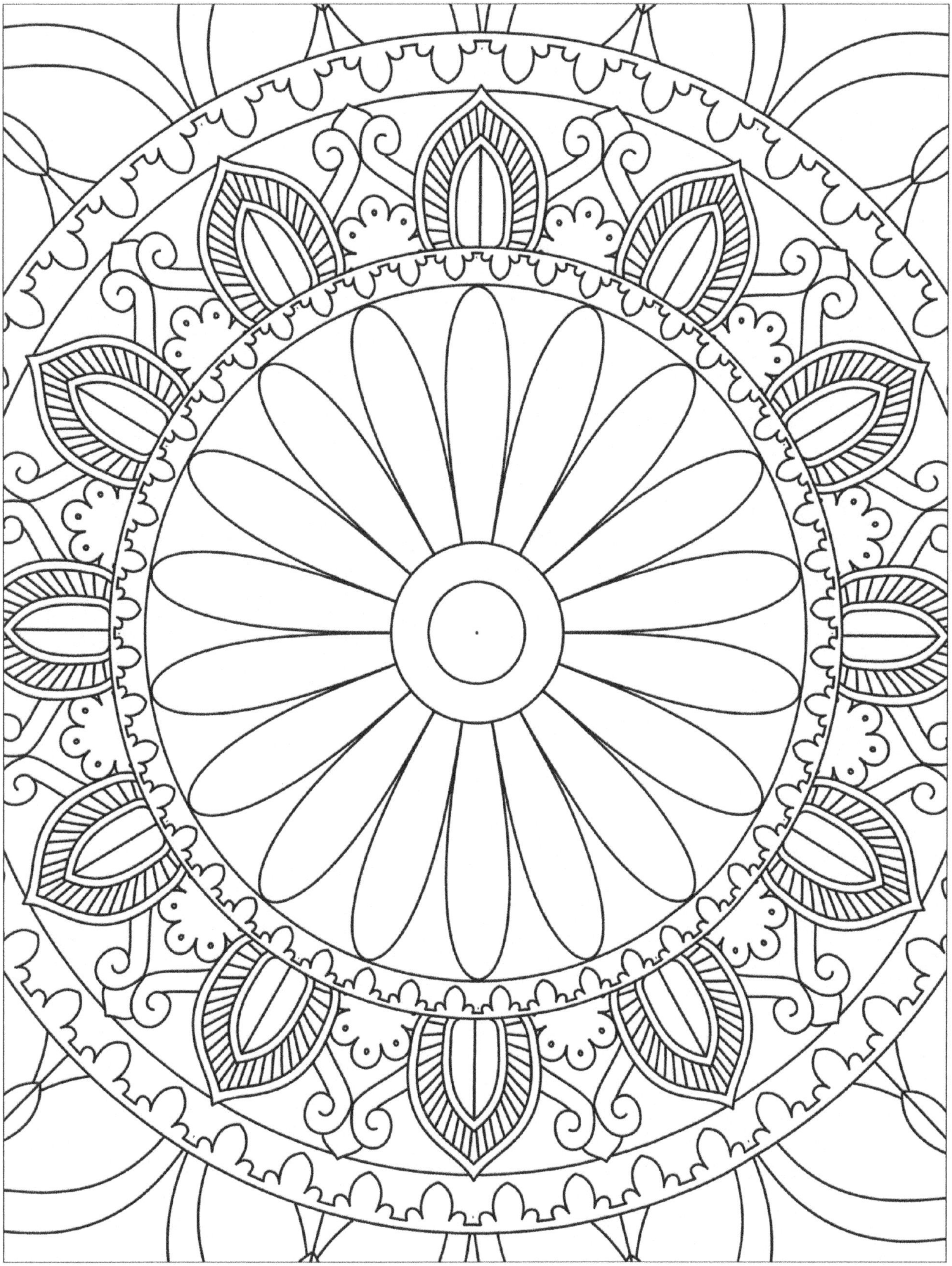

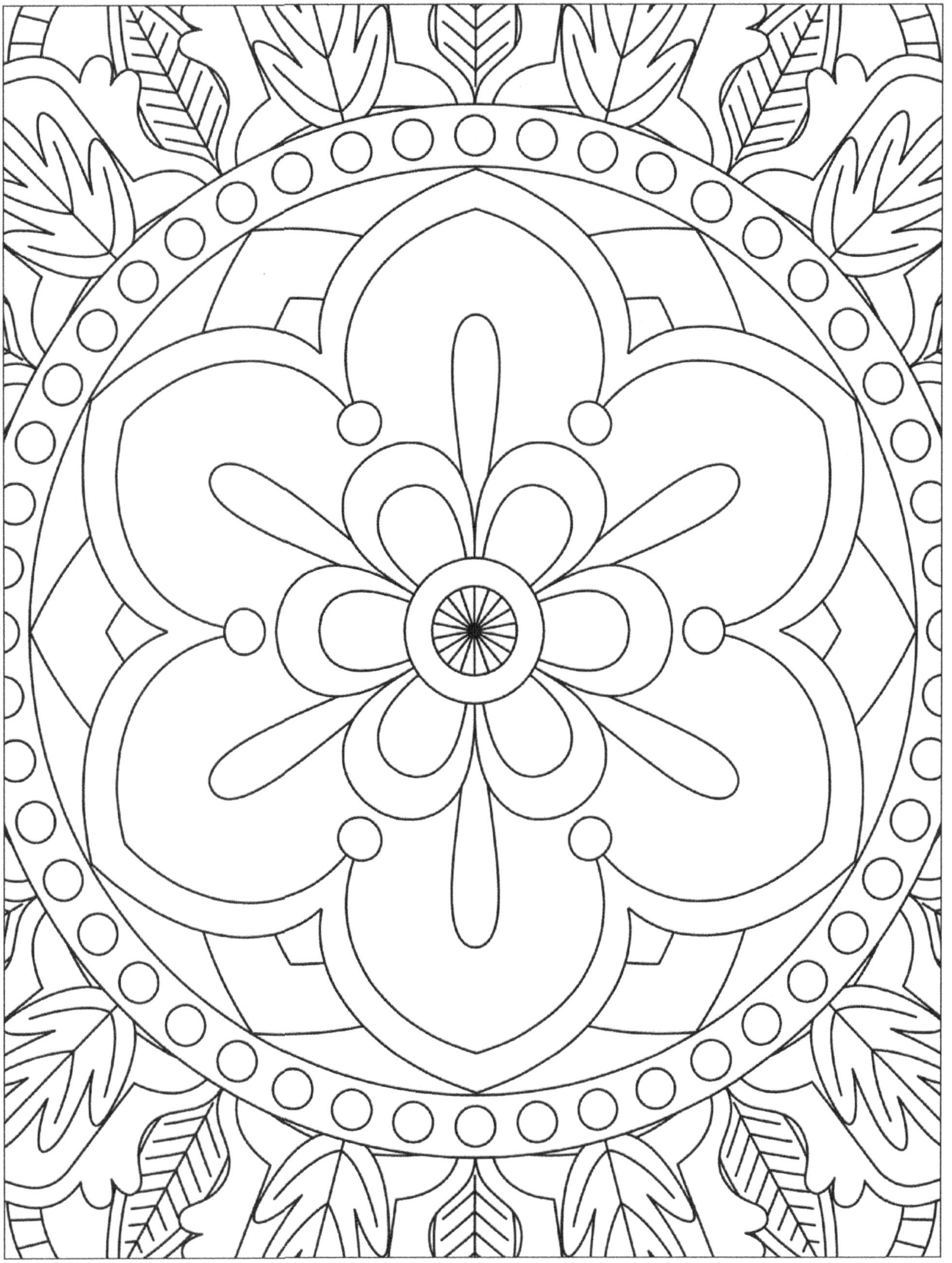

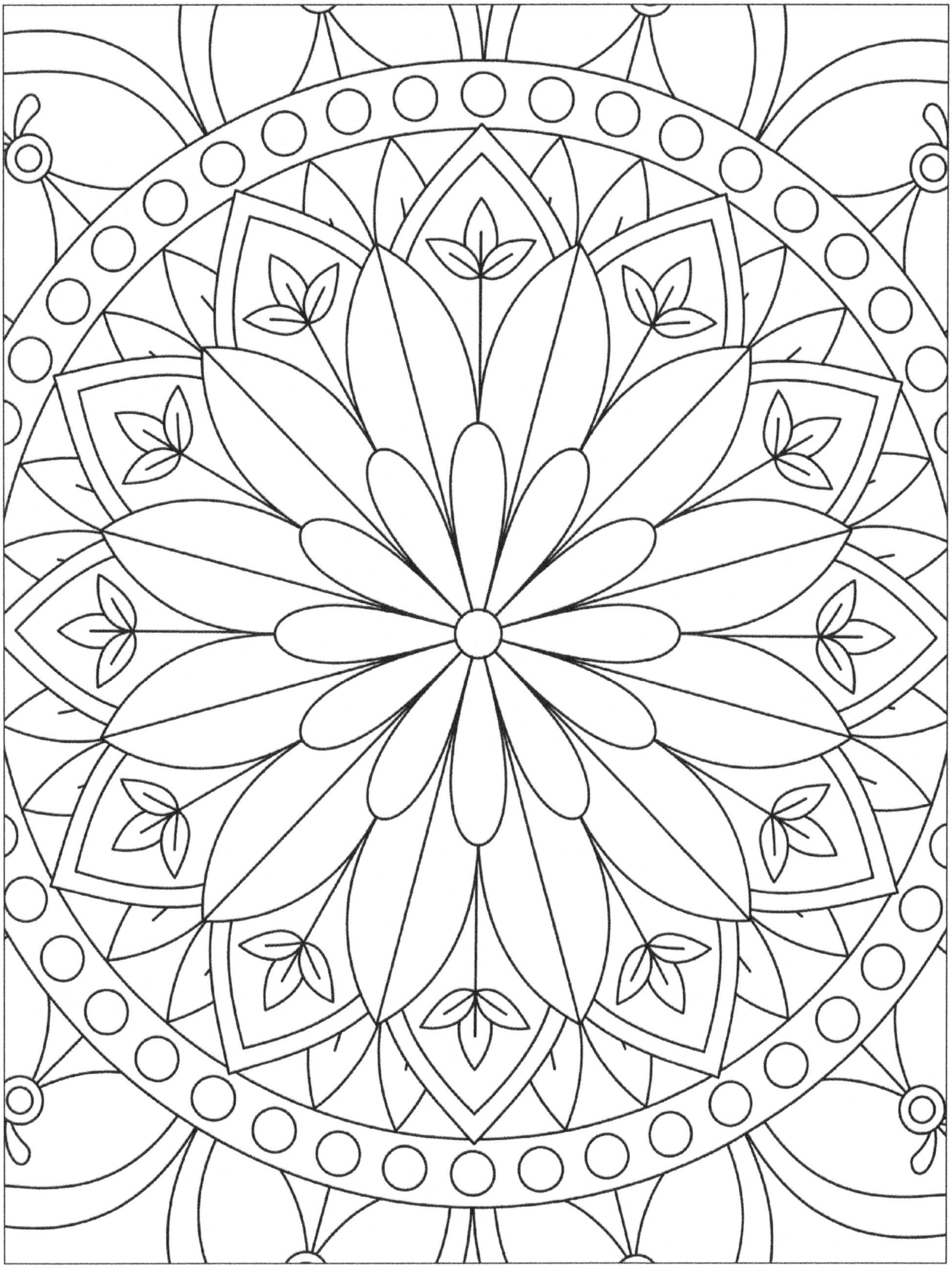

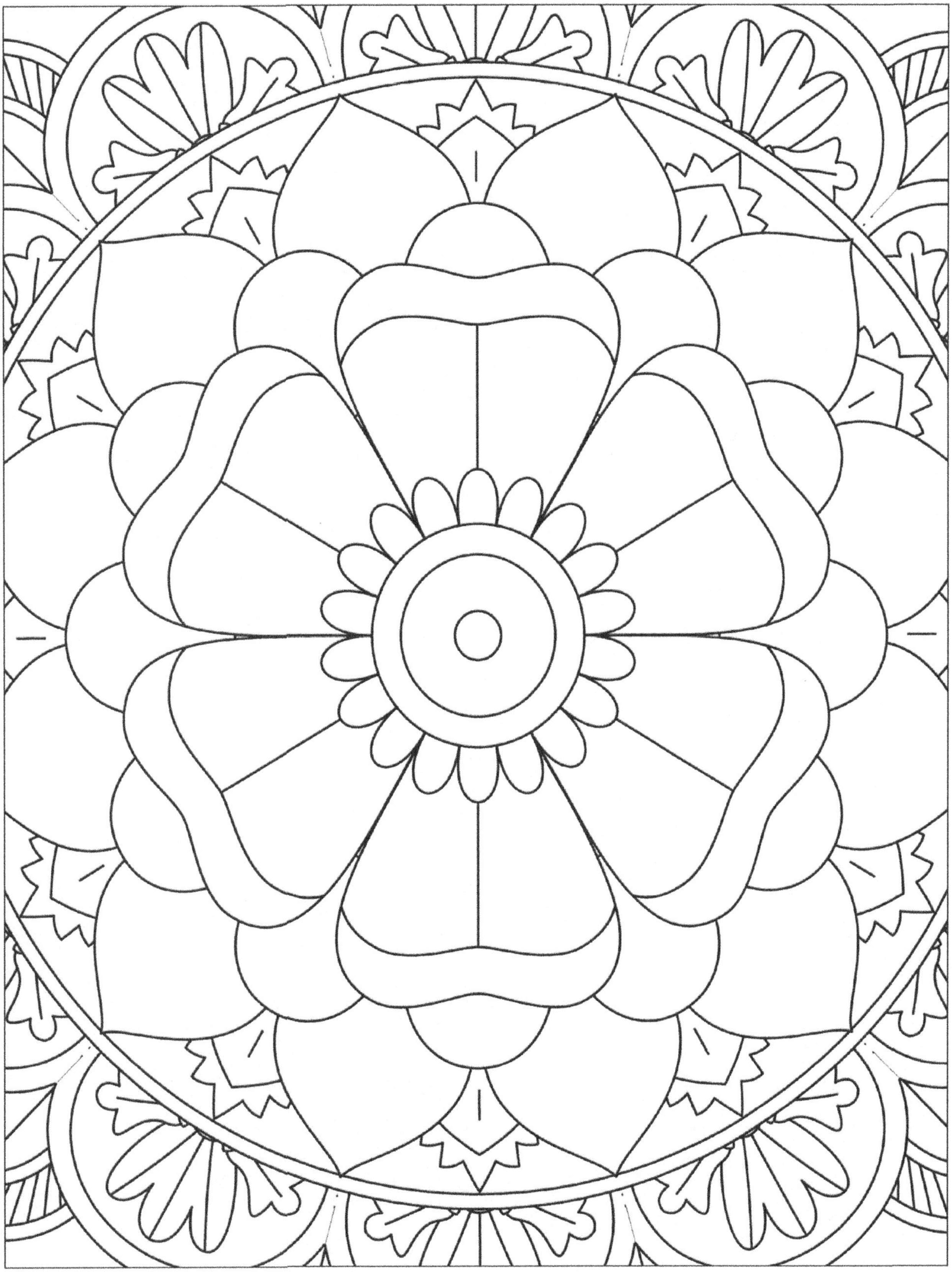

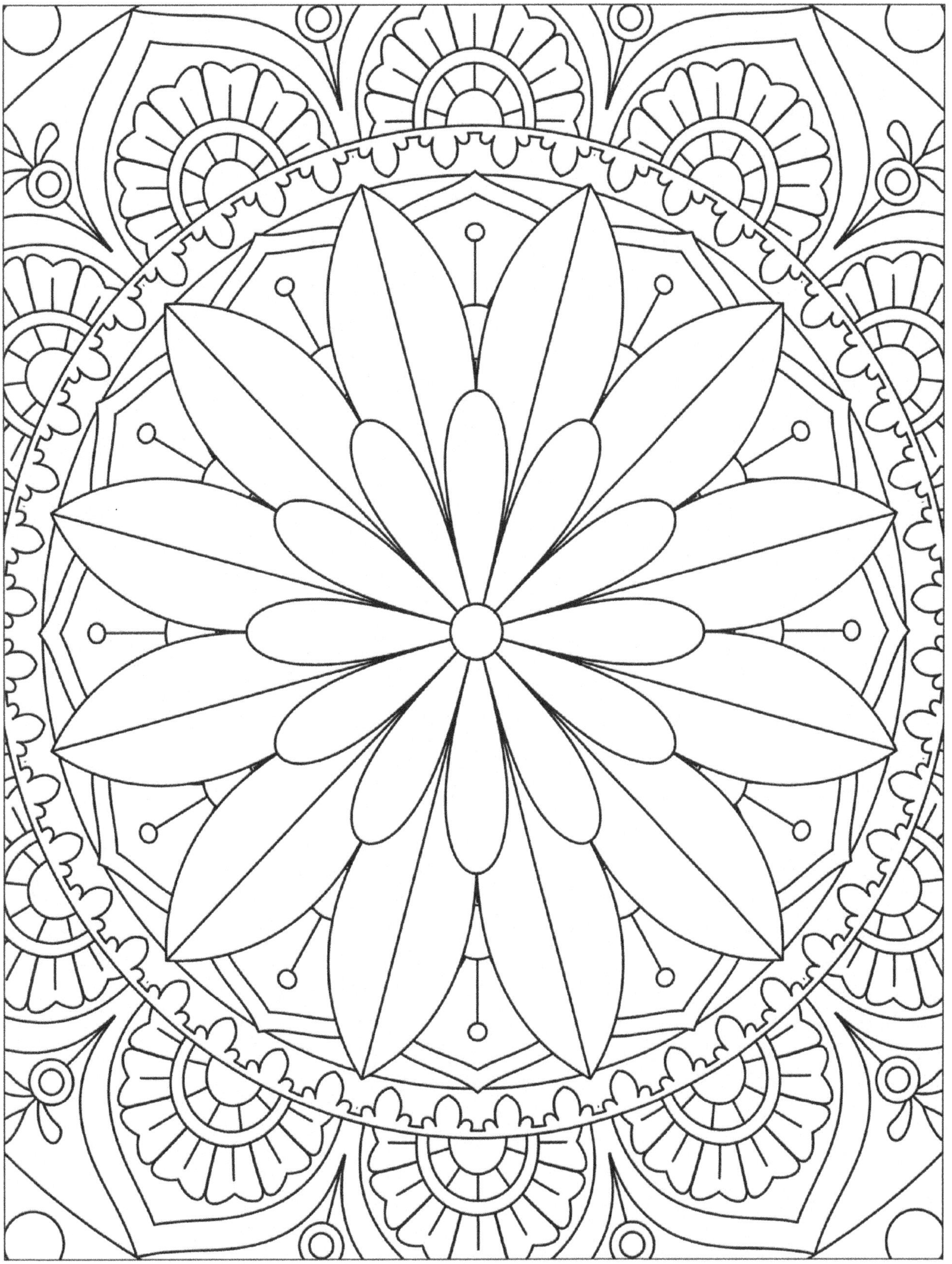

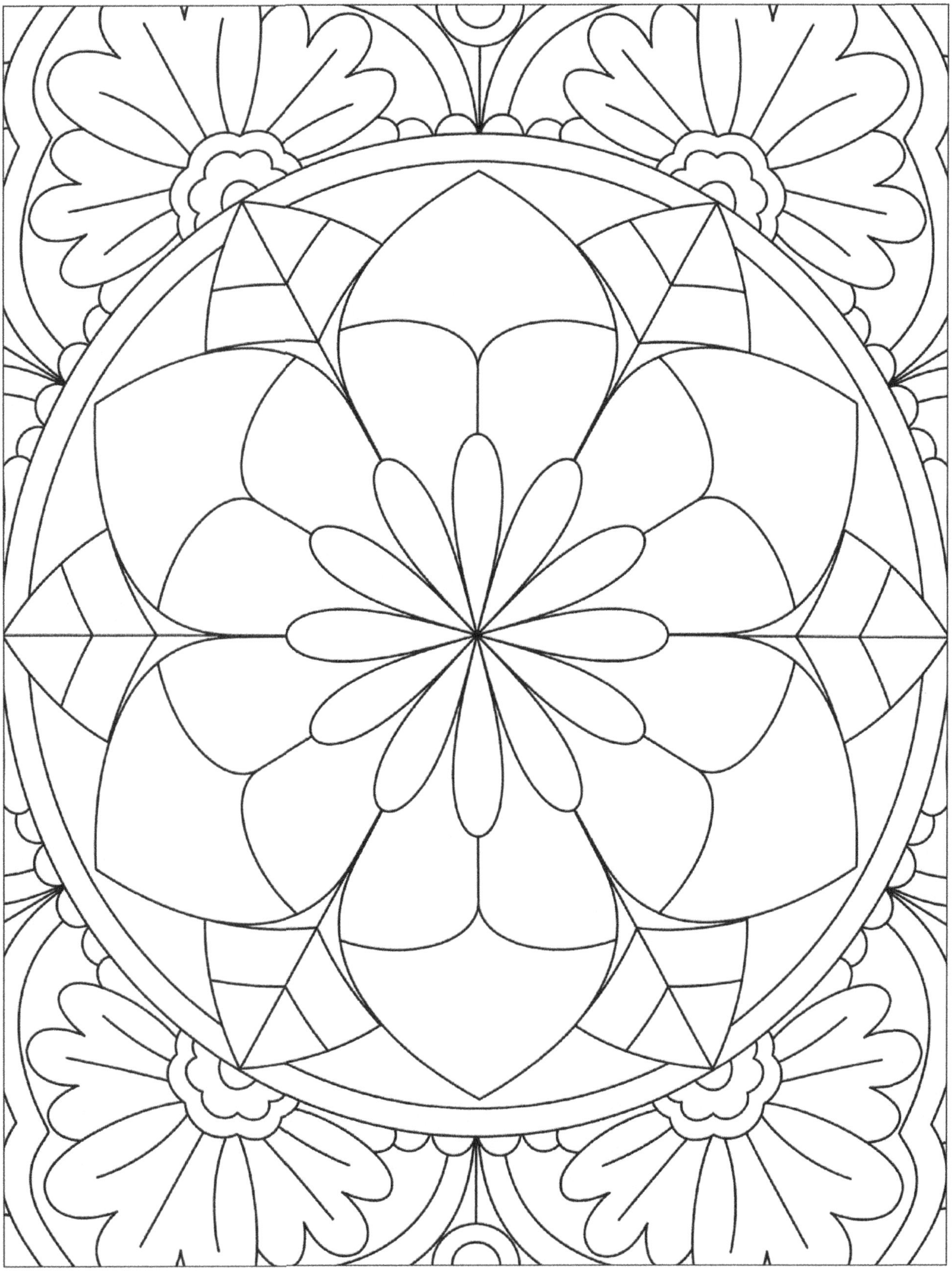

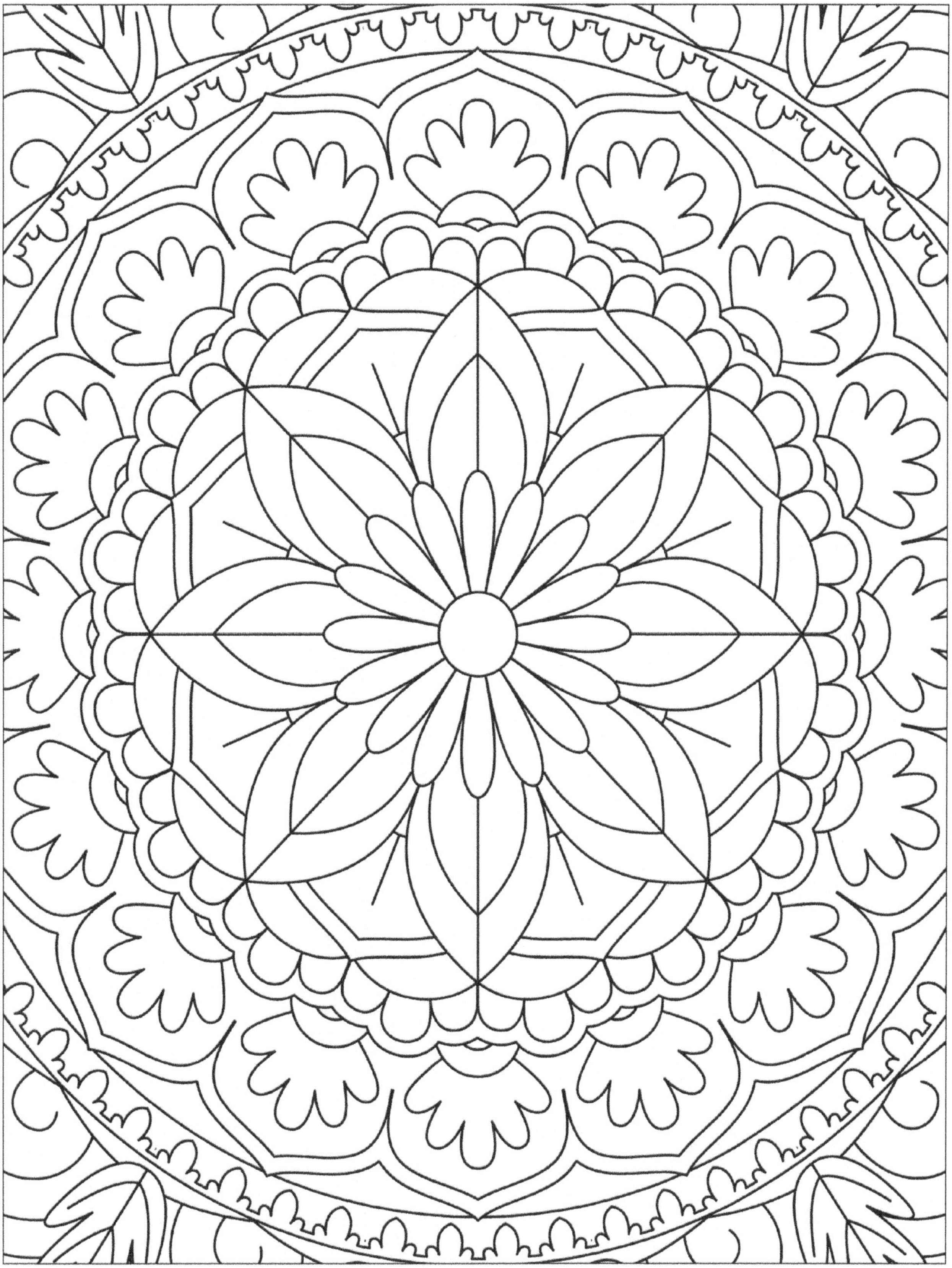

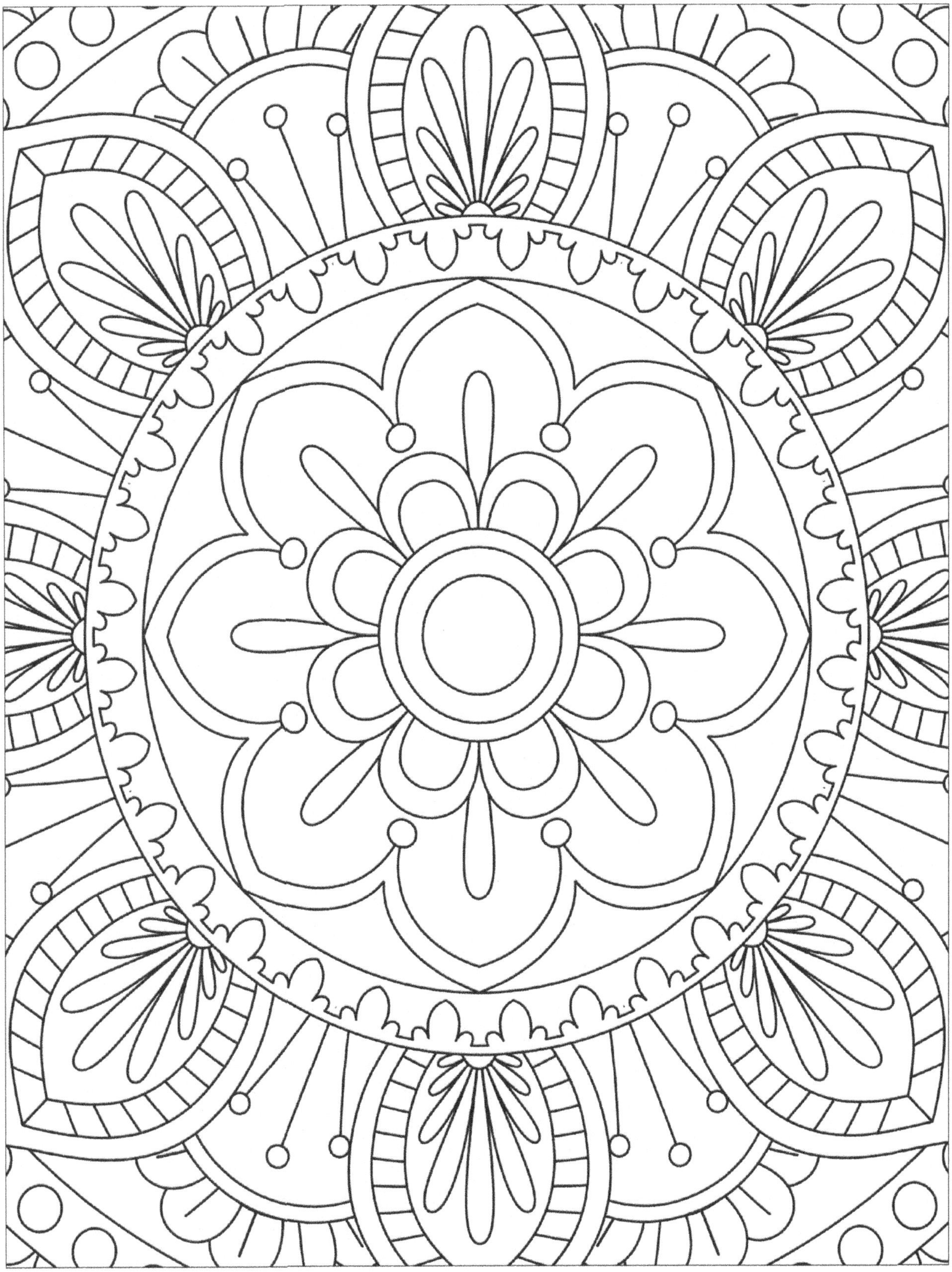

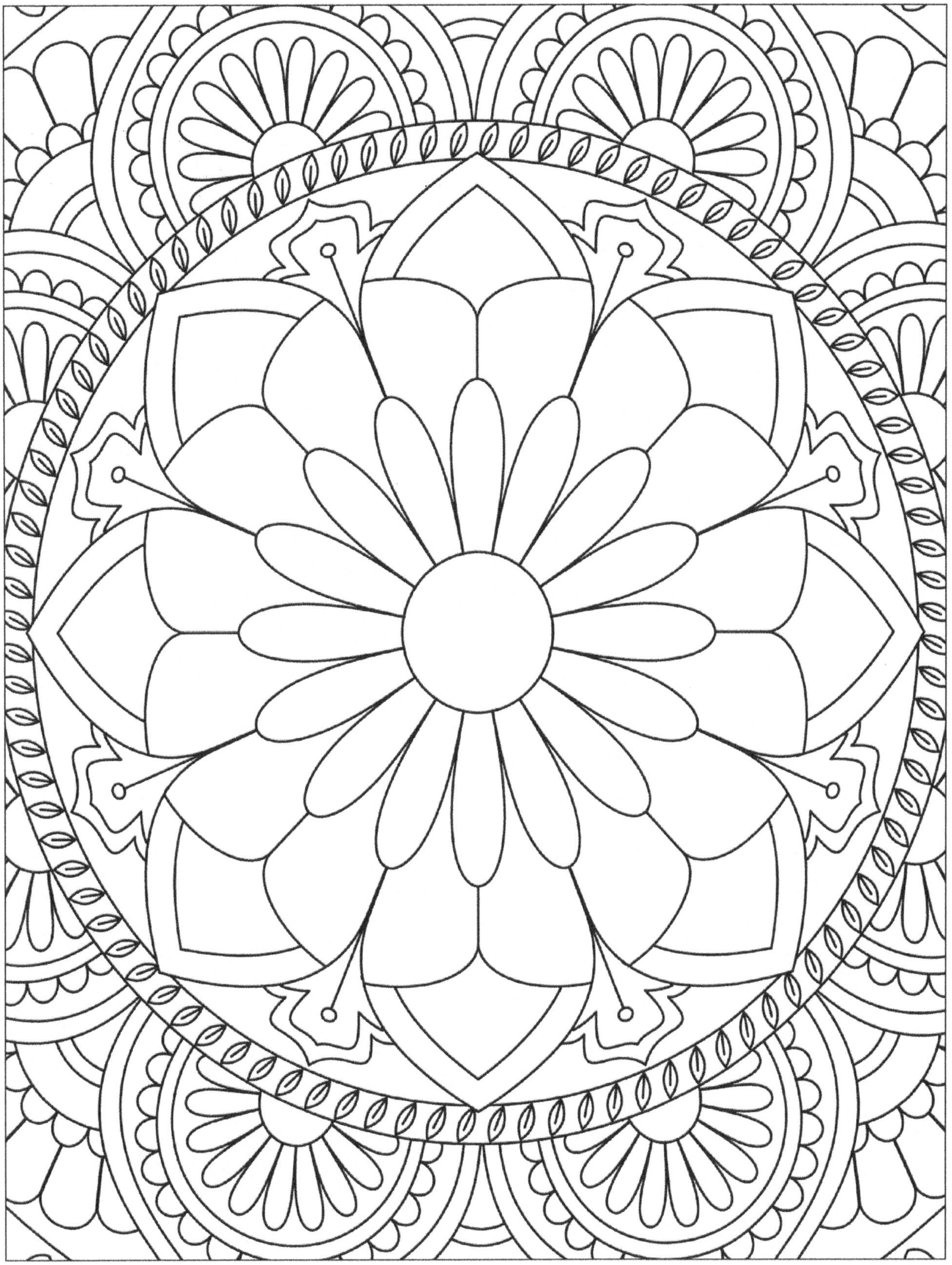

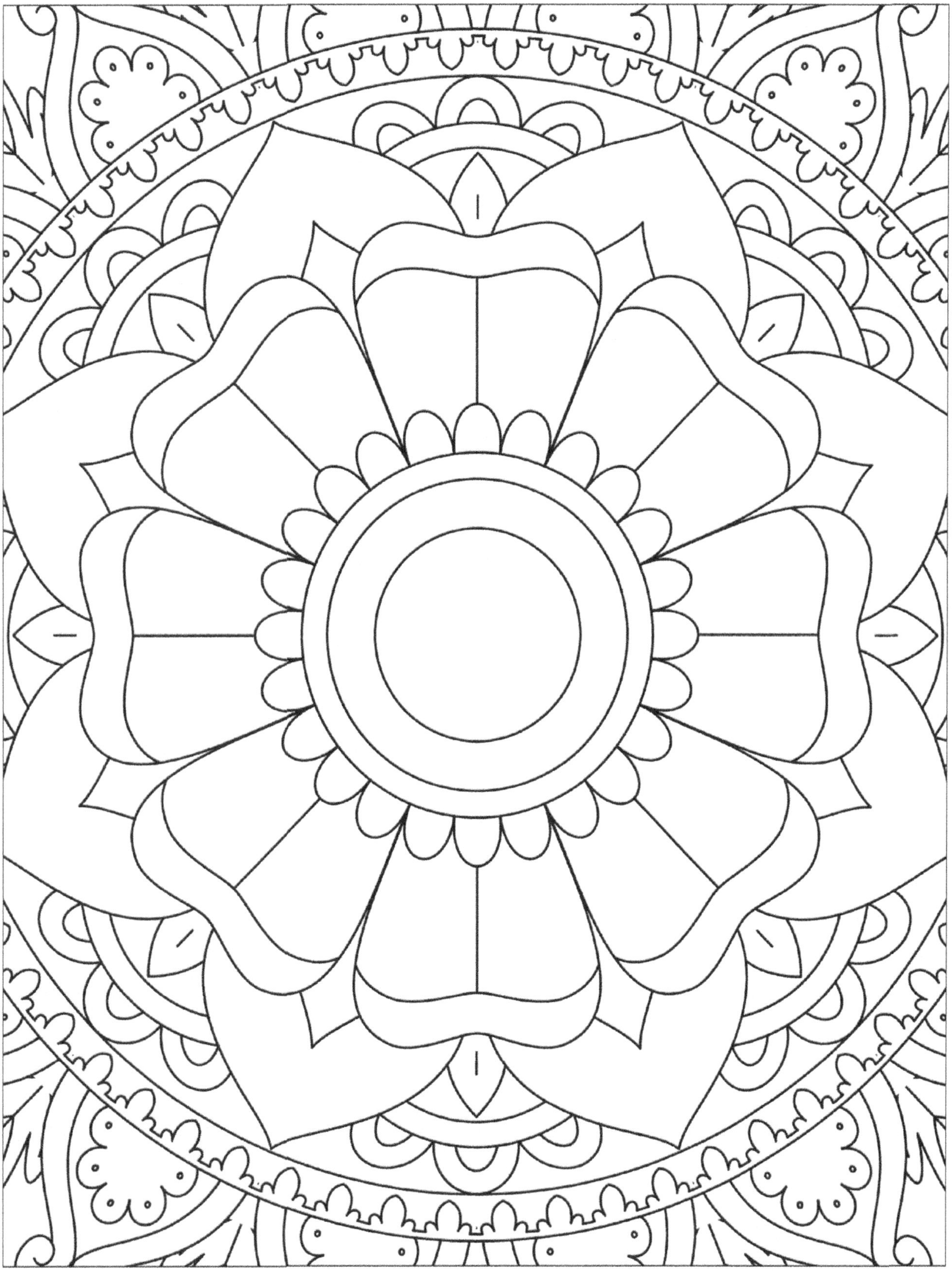

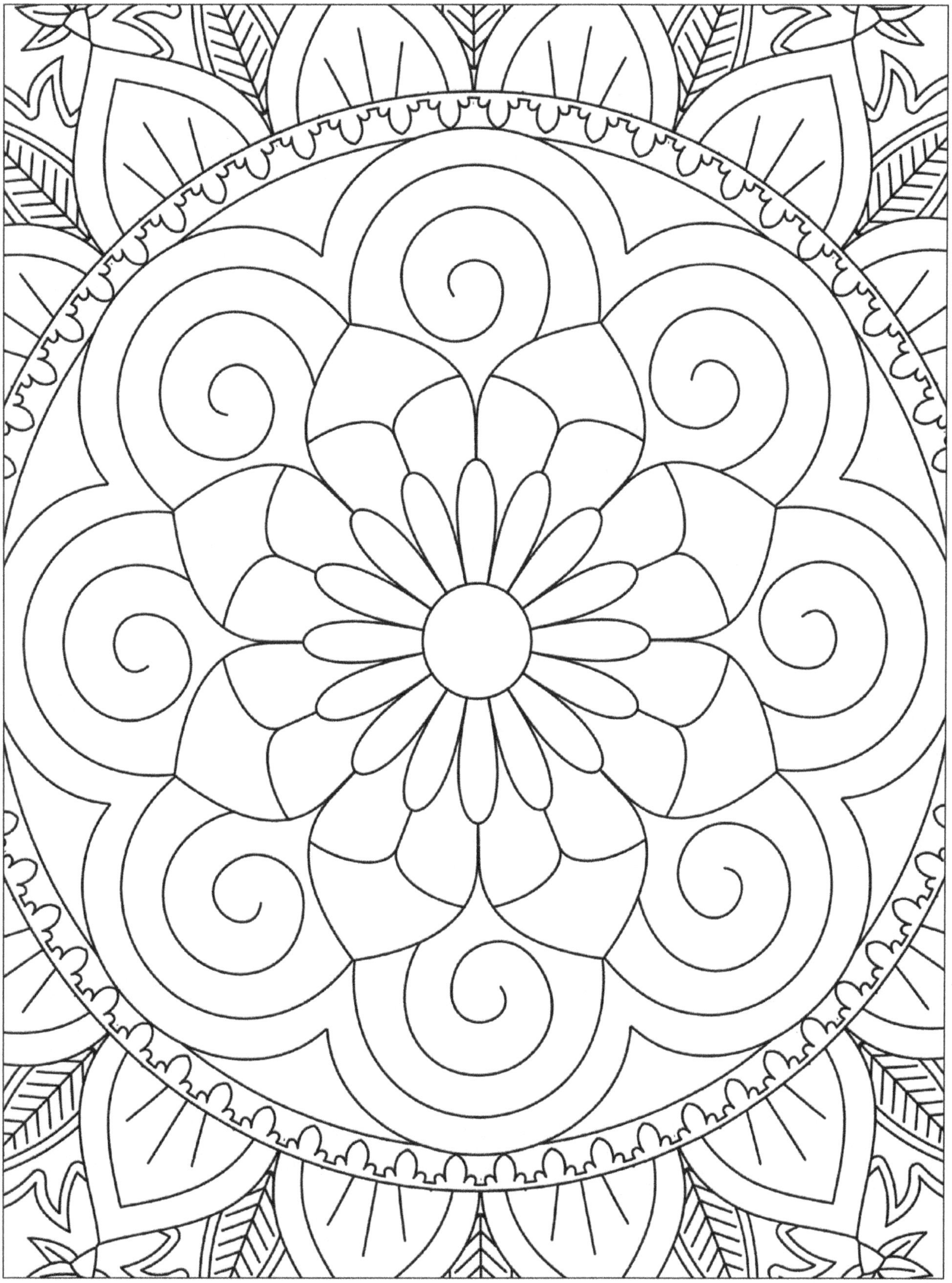

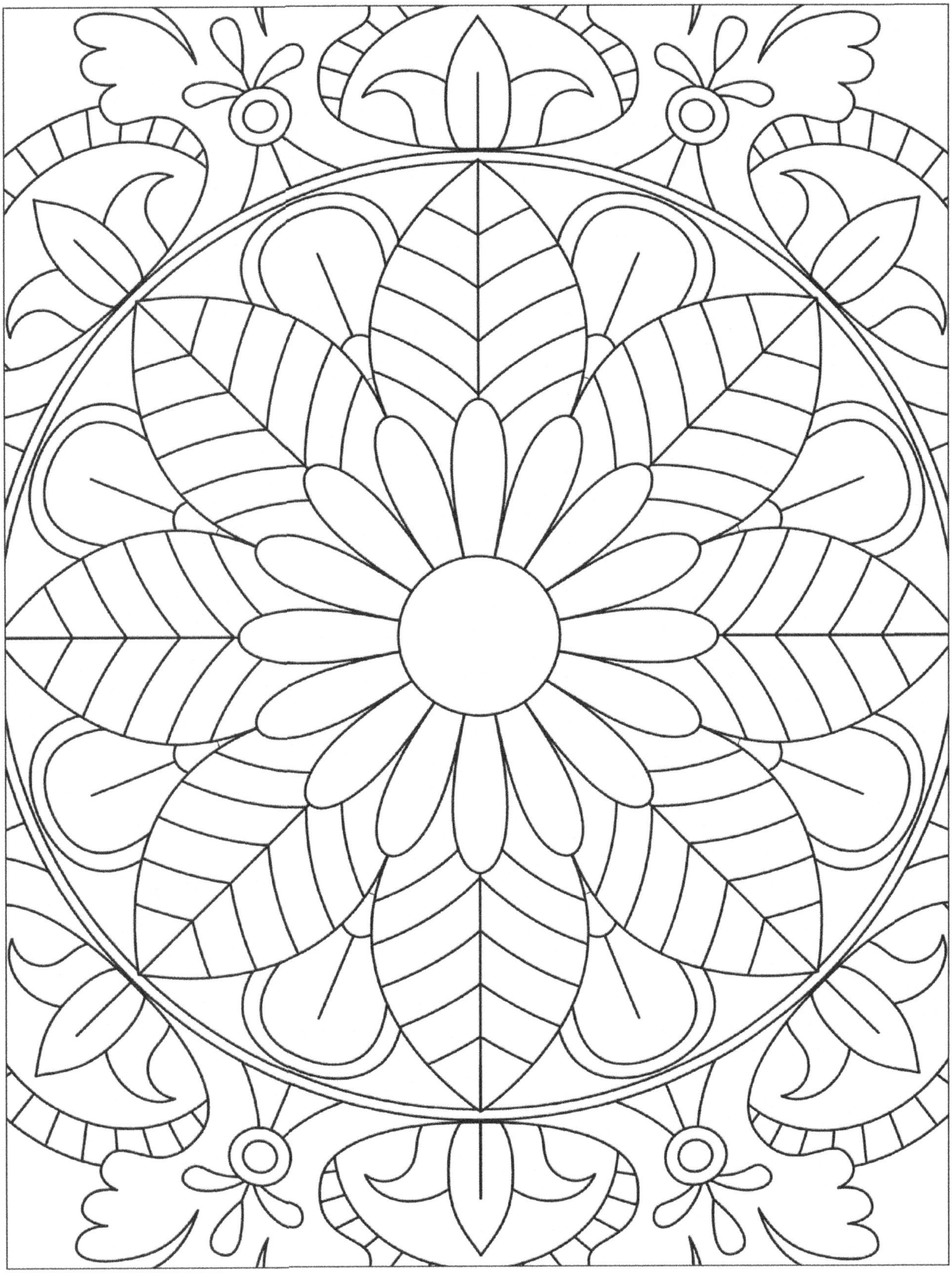

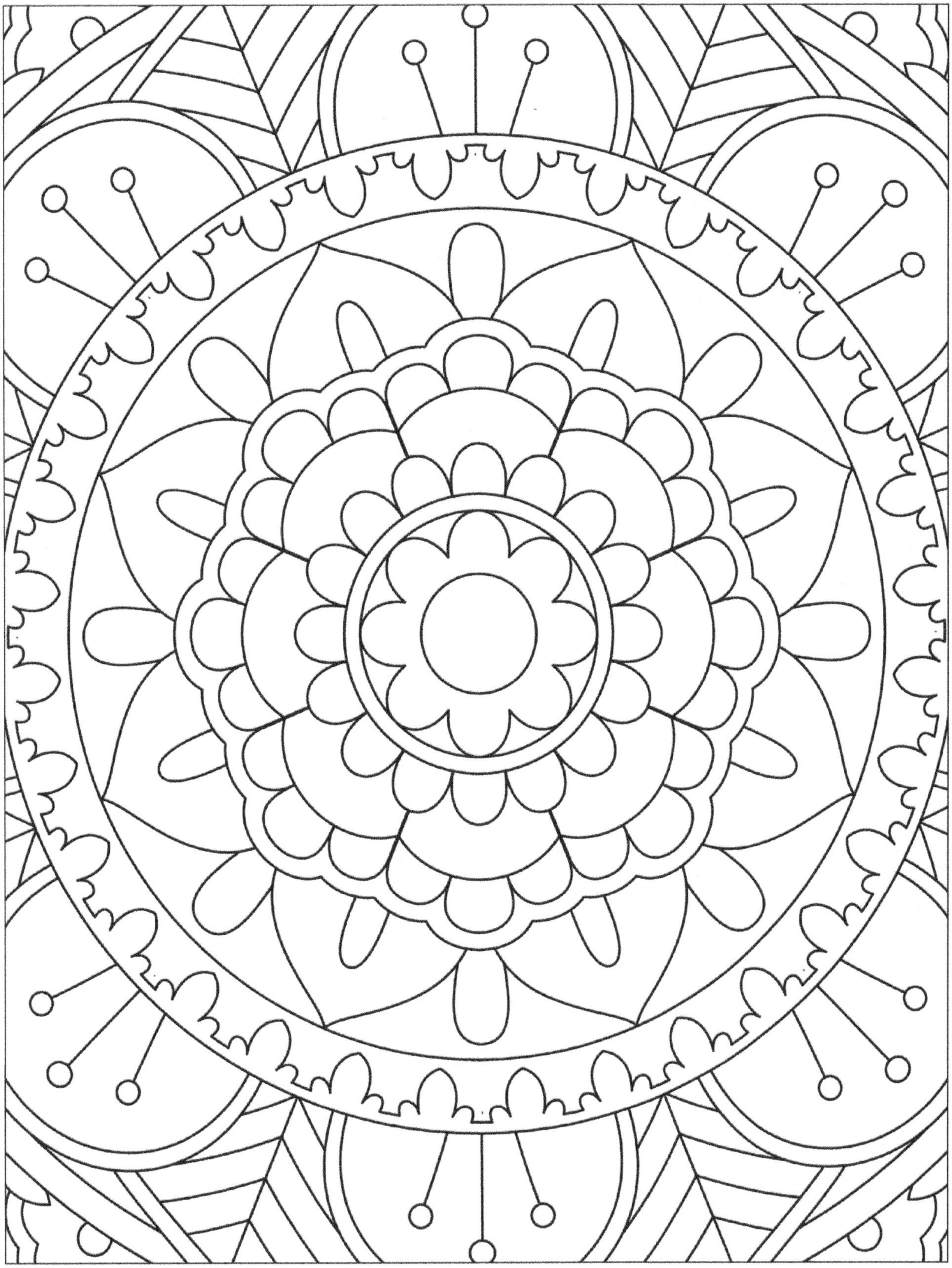

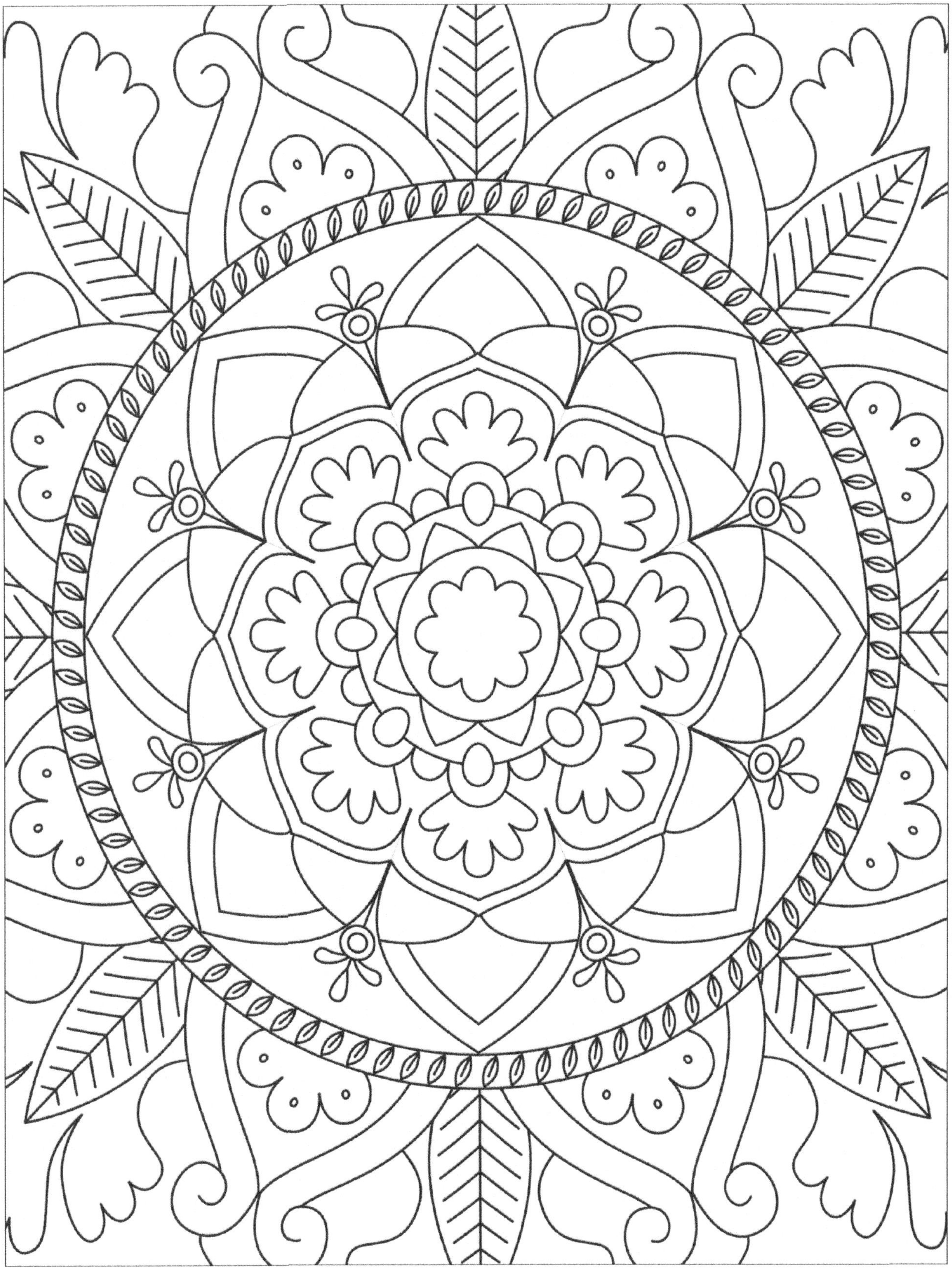

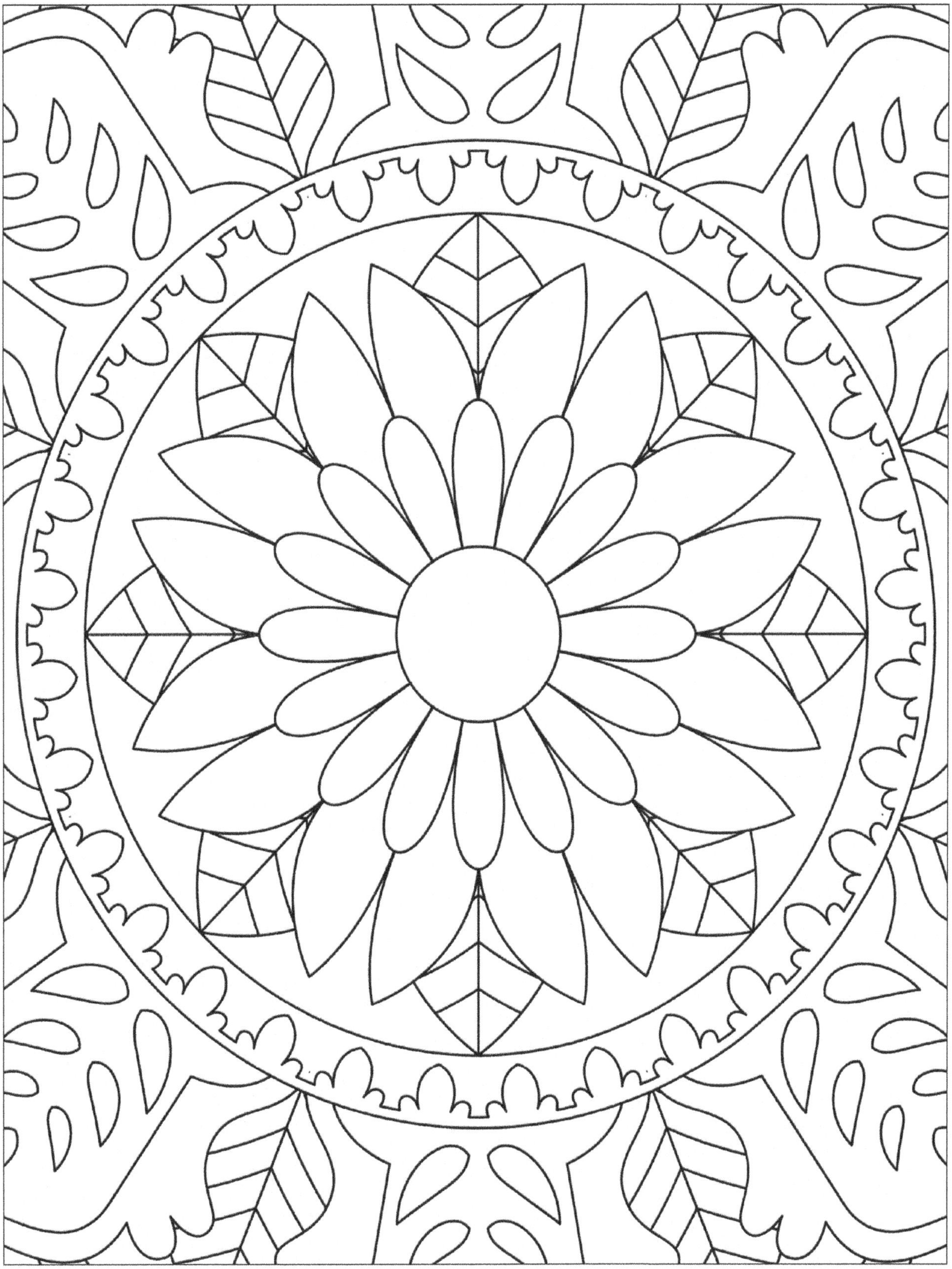

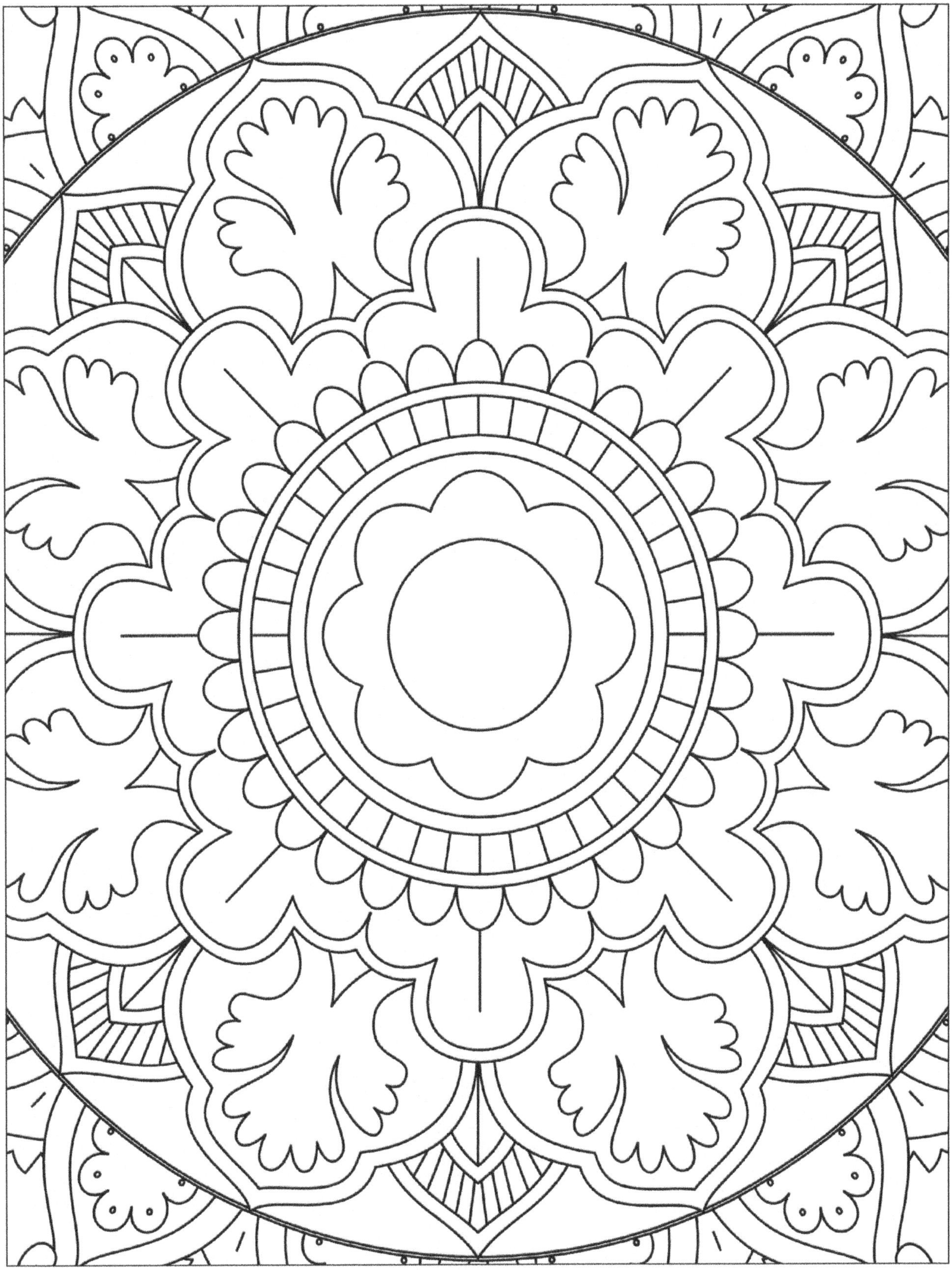

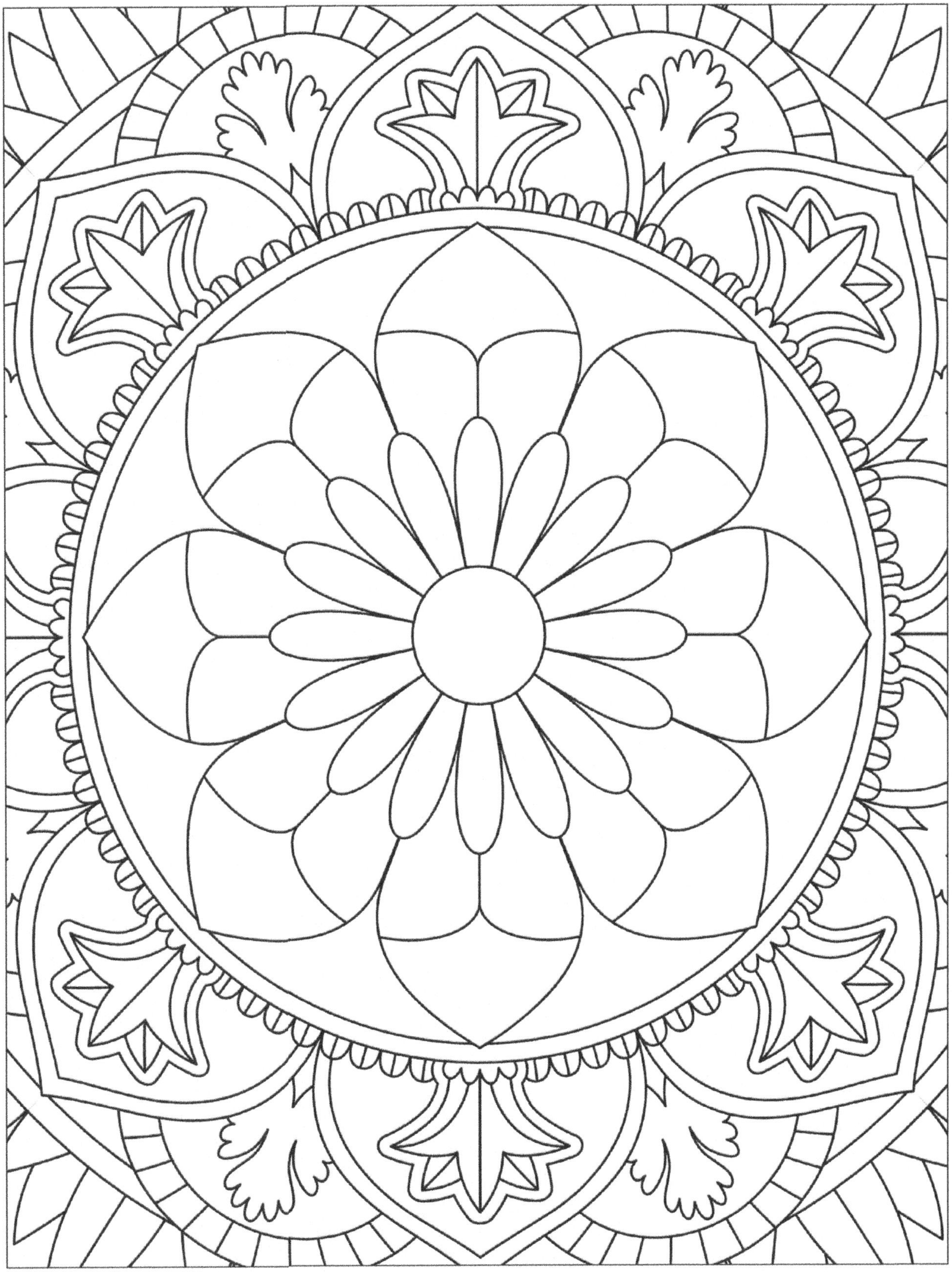

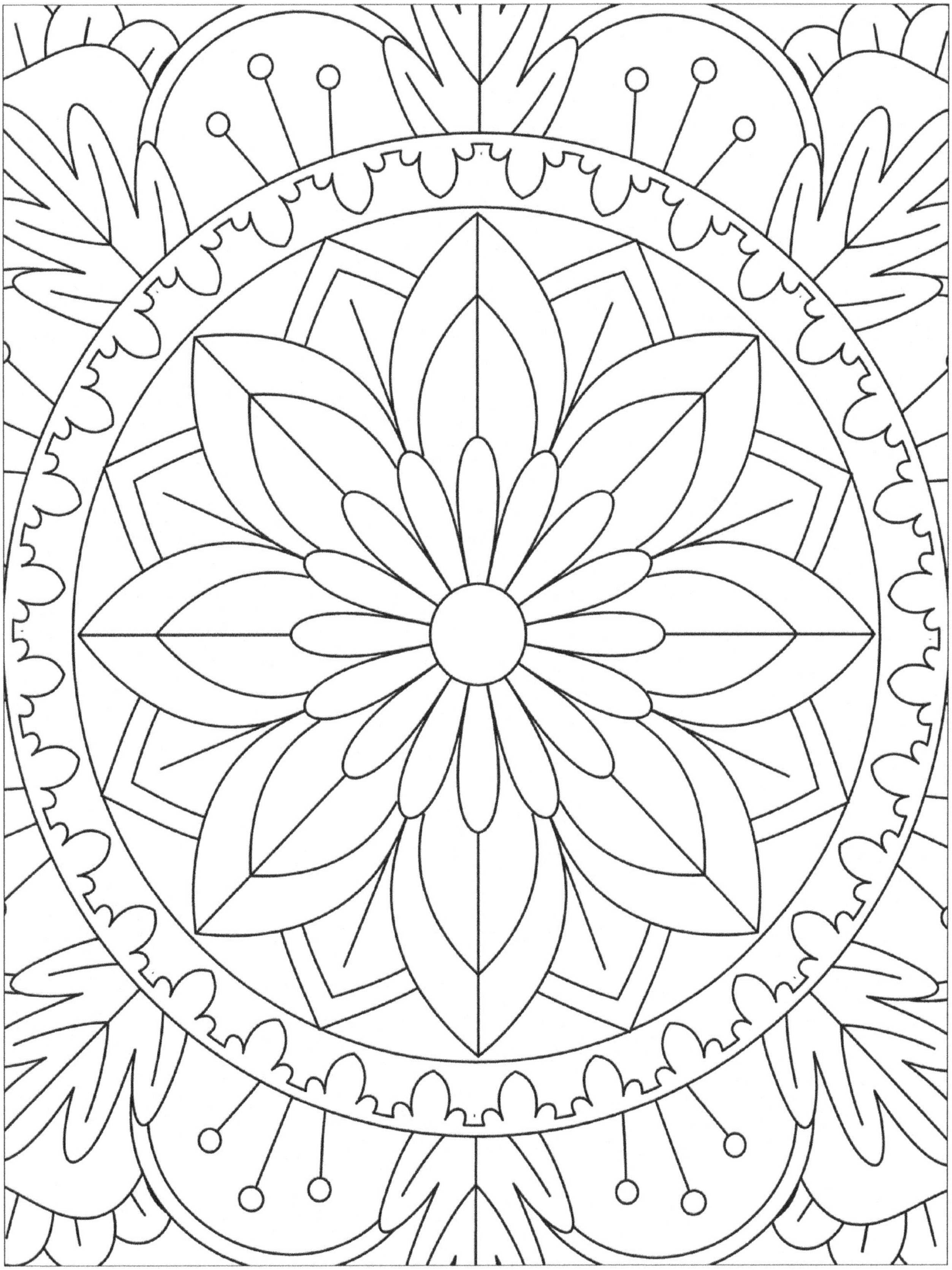

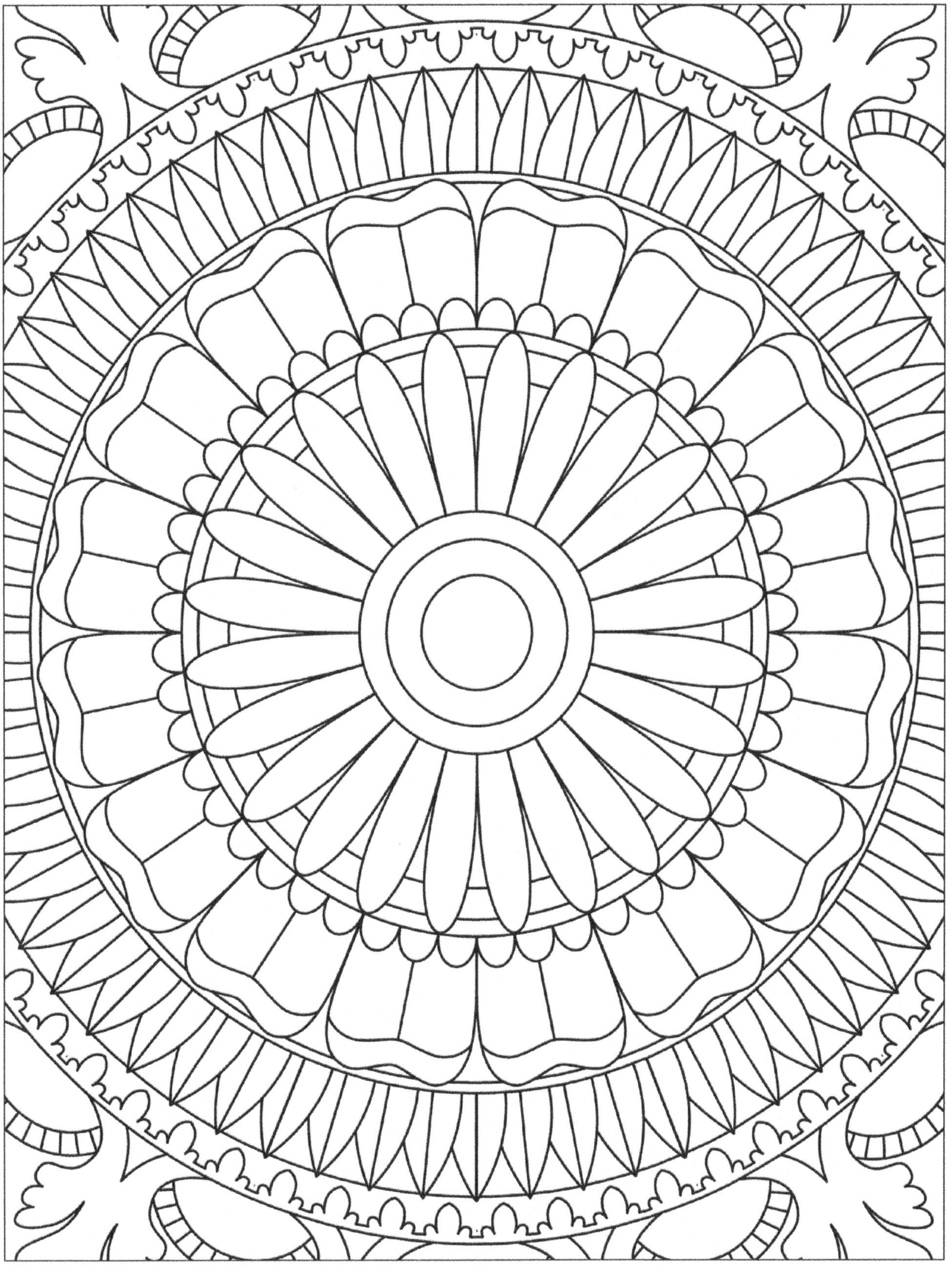

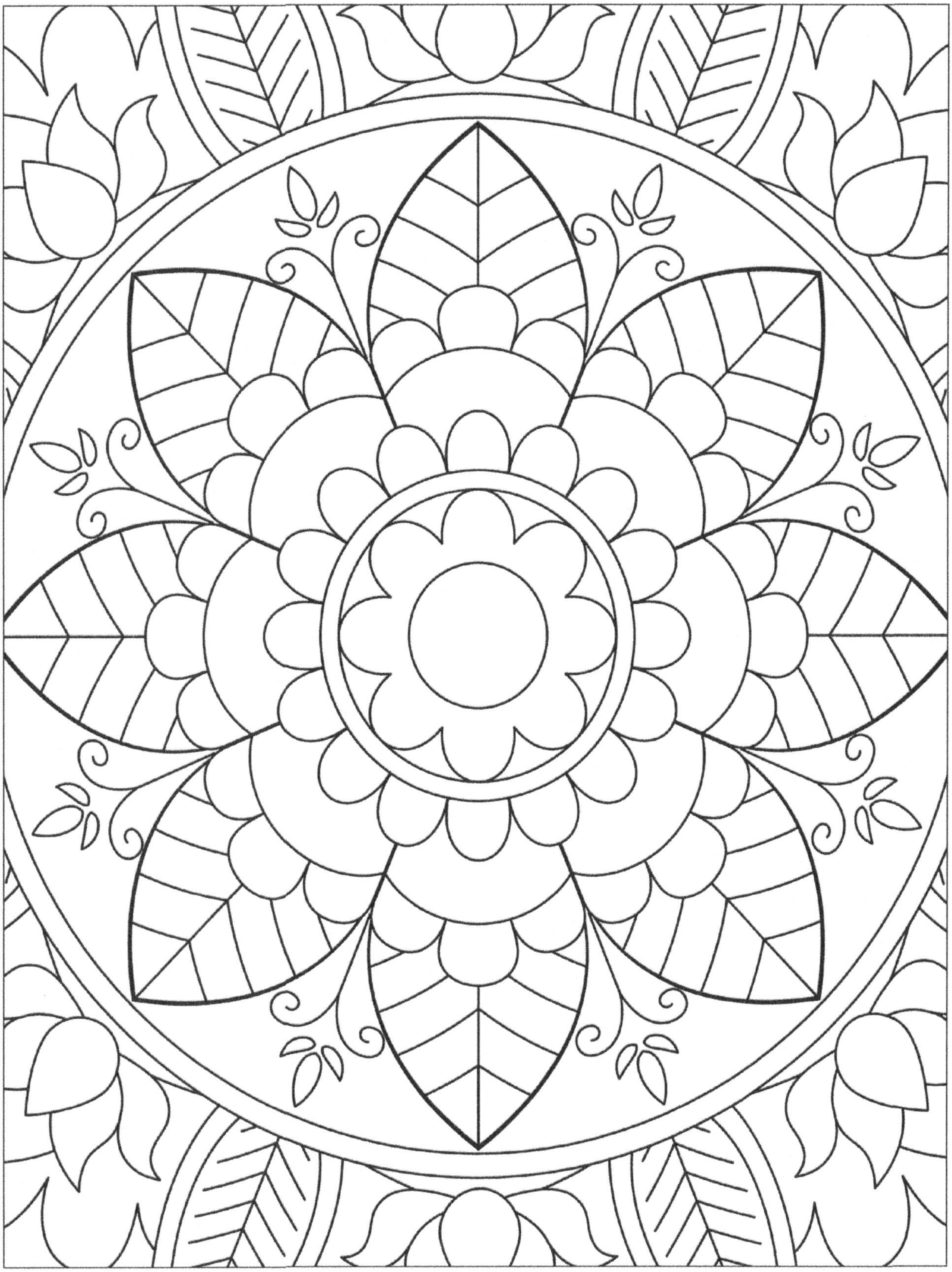

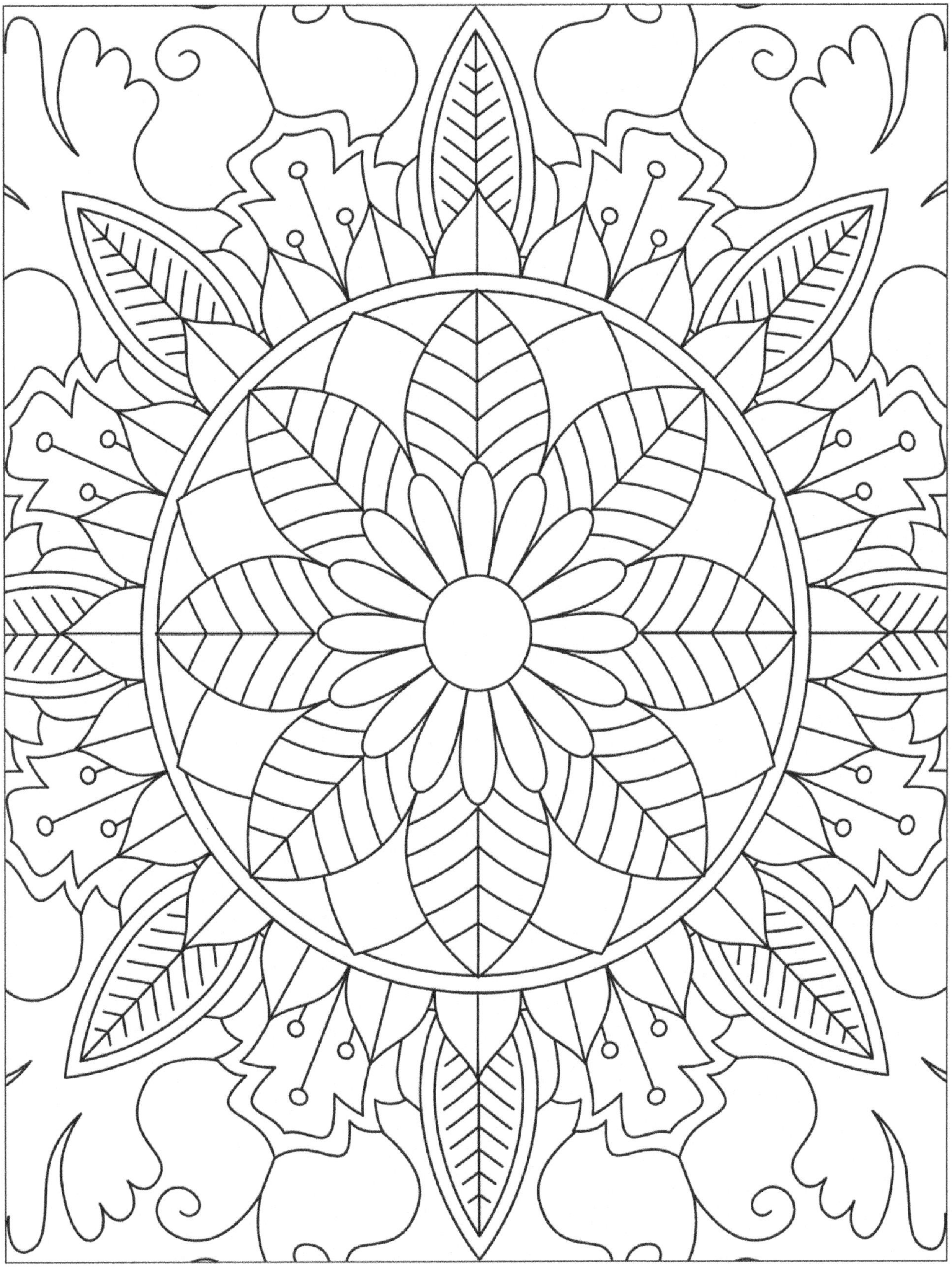

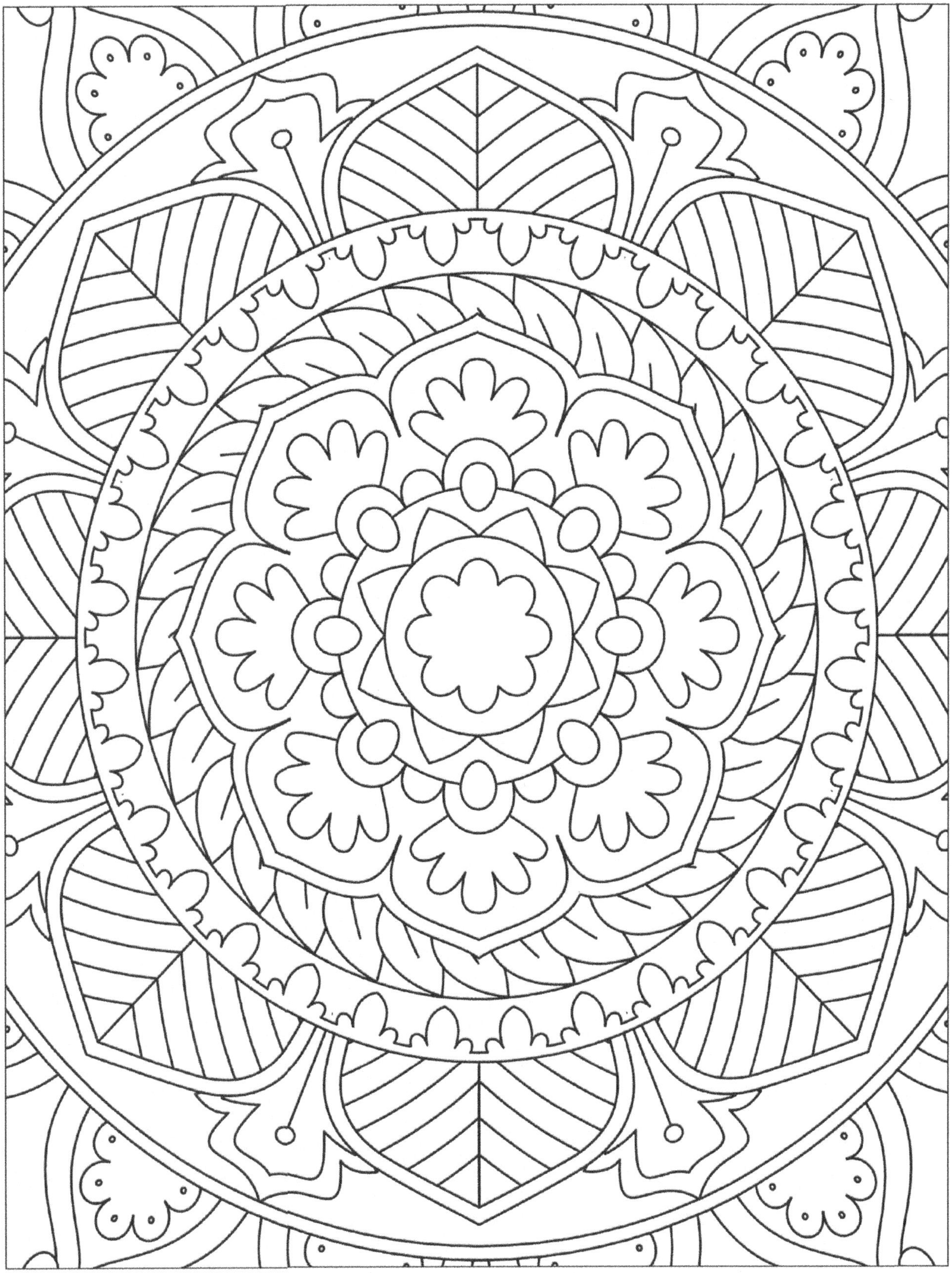

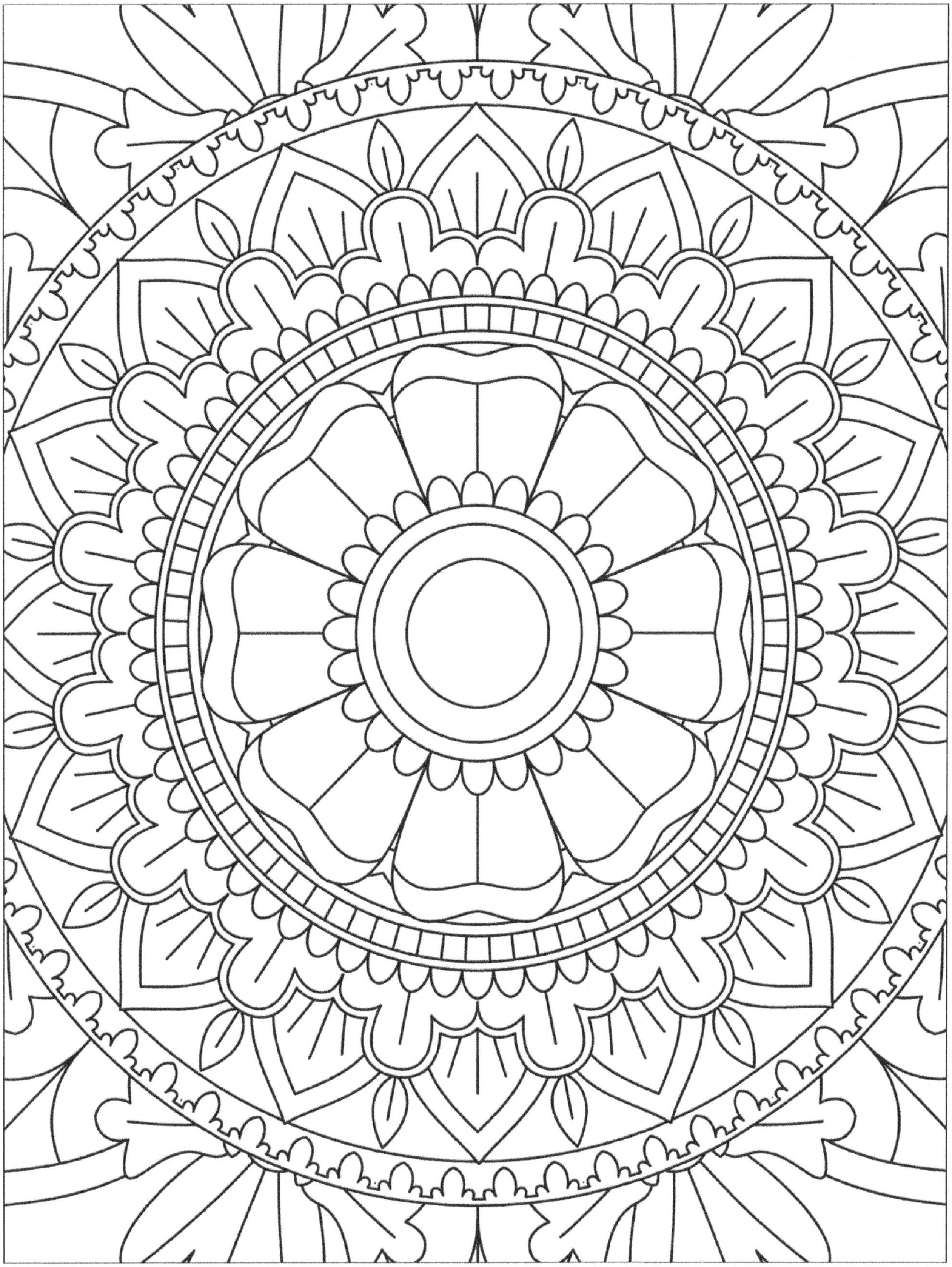

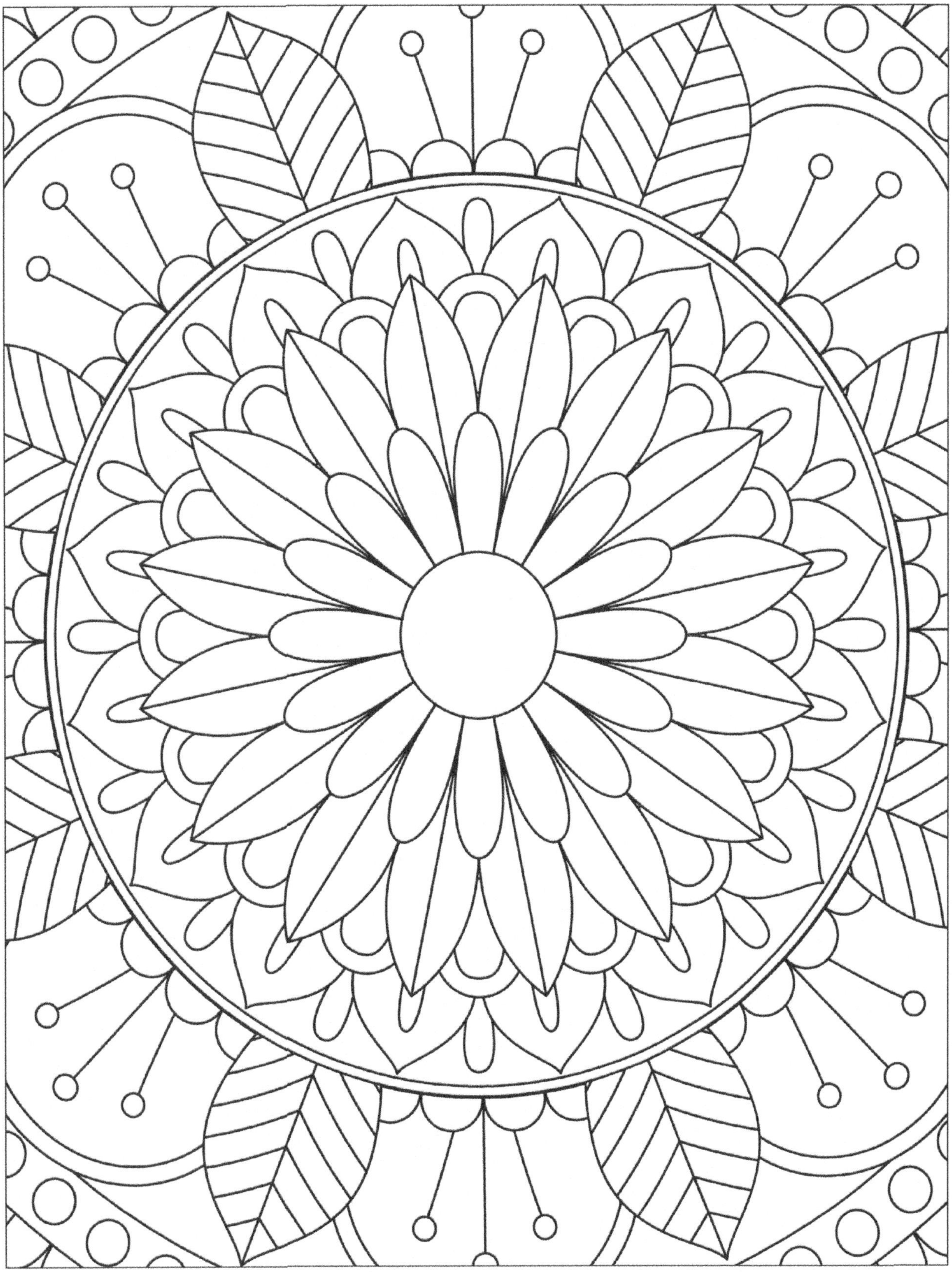

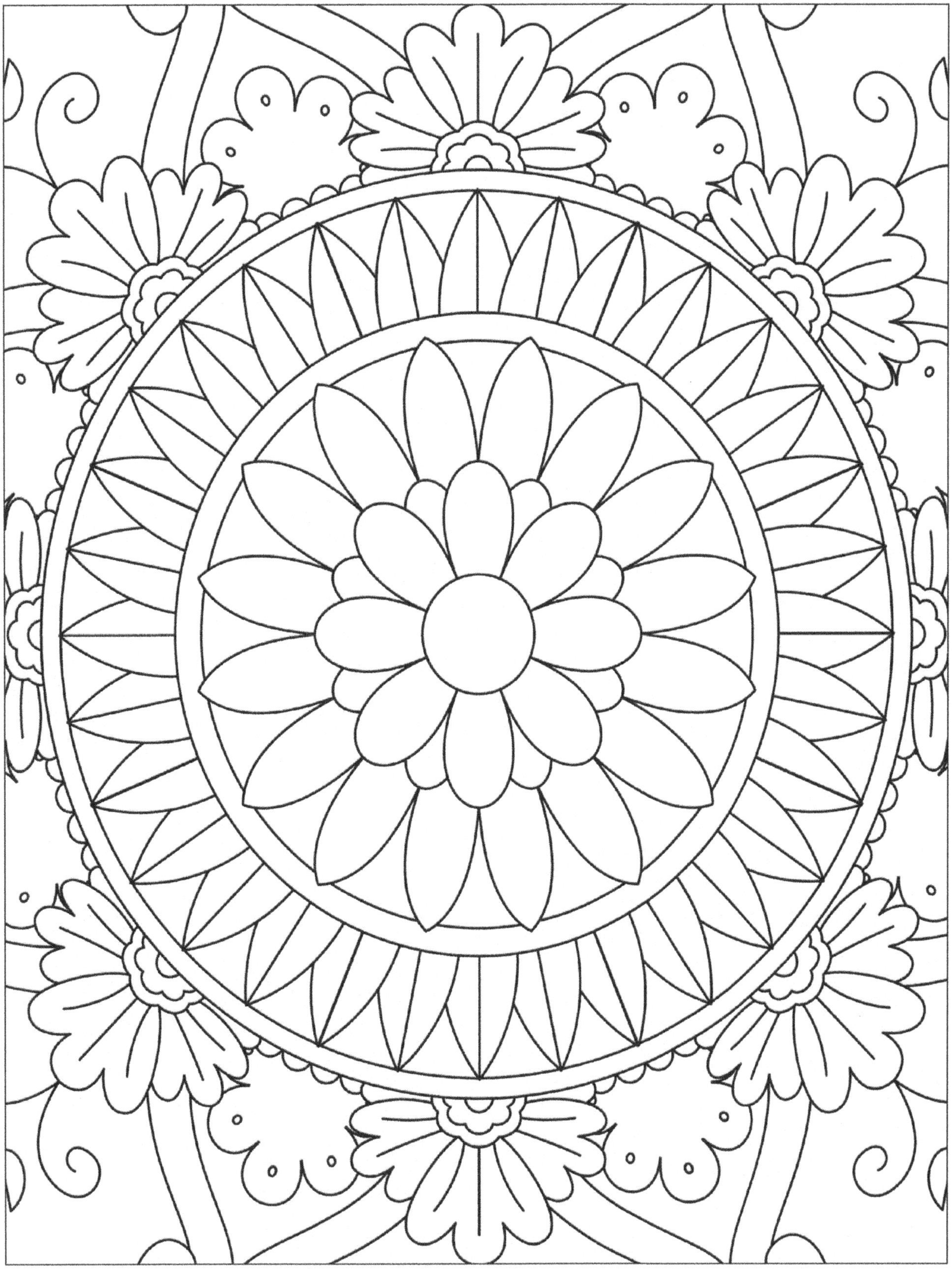

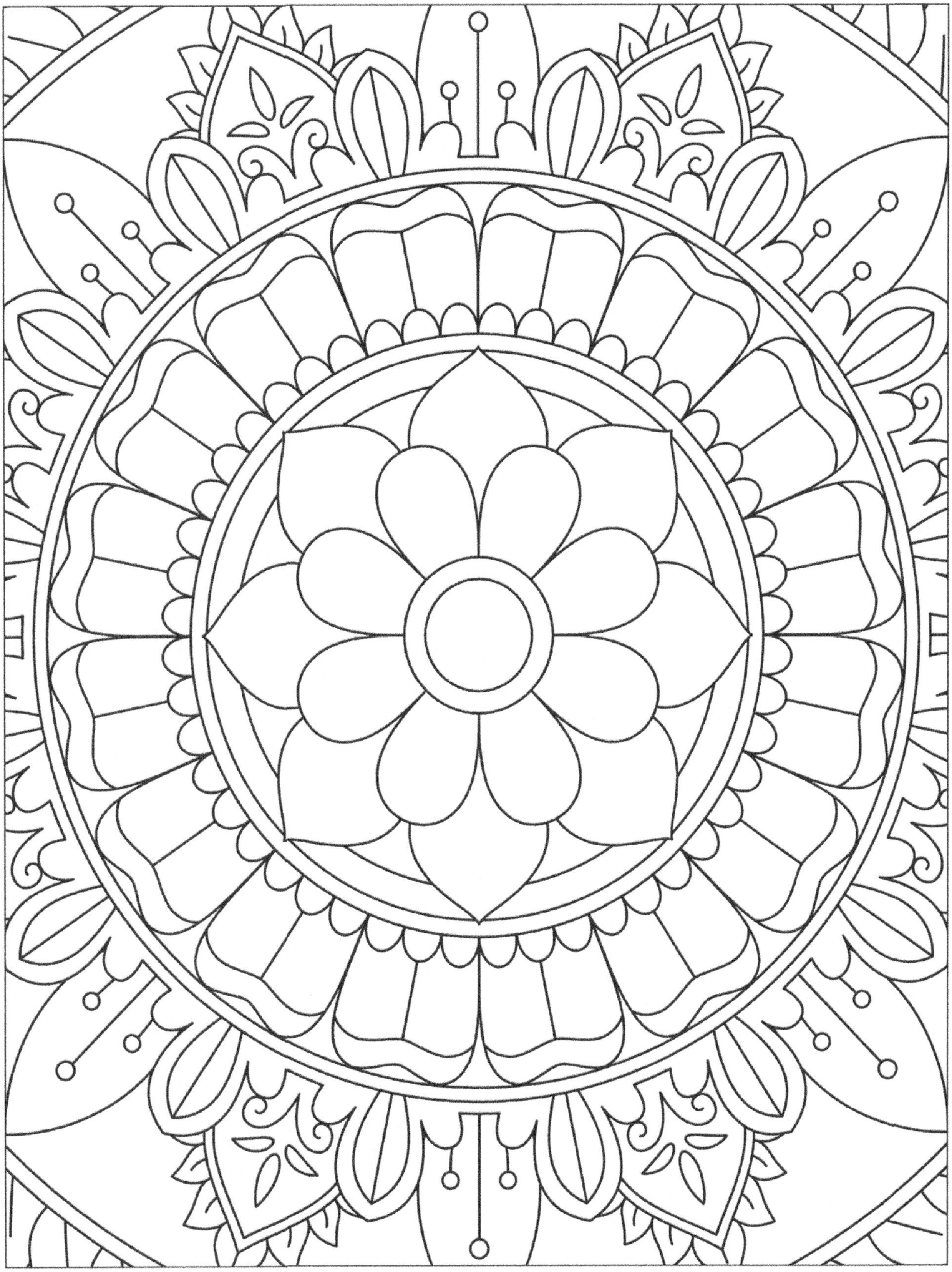

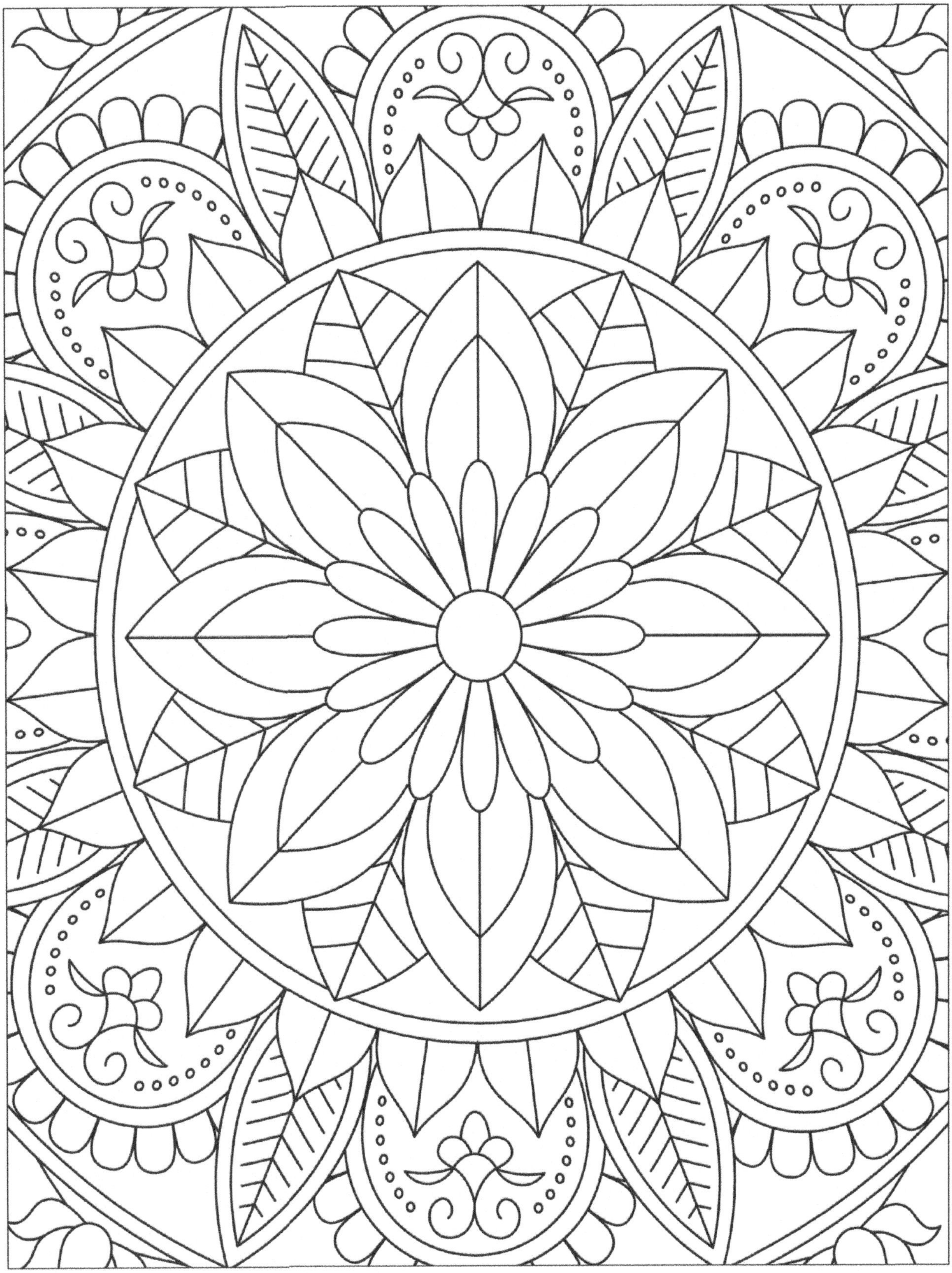